IMAGES
of America

SAUGUS

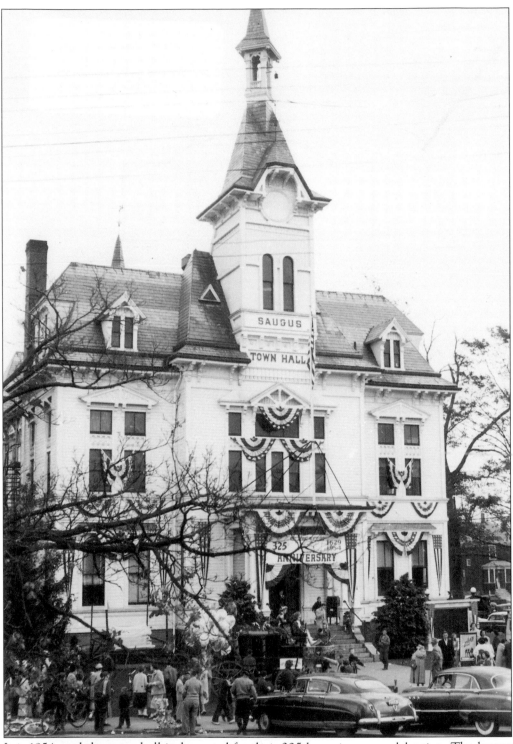

It is 1954, and the town hall is decorated for their 325th anniversary celebration. The largest parade in Saugus history was held on this occasion, and it took three and one-half hours to pass any given spot. (Photograph courtesy of Paul R. Carlson.)

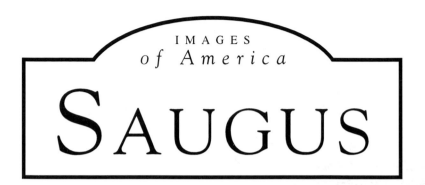

IMAGES
of America

SAUGUS

Norman E. Down

ARCADIA
PUBLISHING

Published by Arcadia Publishing
Charleston, South Carolina

Printed in the United States of America

For all general information contact Arcadia Publishing at:
Telephone 843-853-2070
Fax 843-853-0044
E-mail sales@arcadiapublishing.com
For customer service and orders:
Toll-Free 1-888-313-2665

Visit us on the Internet at www.arcadiapublishing.com

I dedicate this book to the memory of my parents,
who instilled in me a love of learning
and a deep respect for education;
and to my wife Maureen
whose love, wisdom, and guidance
have helped me to realize my potential.

Contents

Acknowledgments   6

Introduction   7

1.   Buildings and Neighborhoods   9

2.   Men in Uniform: Police, Fire, and Military   23

3.   Churches   35

4.   Stores, Industries, and Businesses   45

5.   That's Entertainment   57

6.   Schools   71

7.   The Rustic Life   83

8.   Transportation: Way to Go   95

9.   People   107

10. The Newburyport Turnpike: Route One   115

Acknowledgments

In 1975, the late Helen Cutter approached me about doing a Saugus project for the upcoming Bicentennial year. She felt it was important that the people of Saugus share her knowledge of the town's rich history. Accordingly, she gathered photographs from every person and source she could find. My job was to copy the prints into slides. The agreement was that she would get one copy and I would keep one. Unfortunately, I never met many of the people who lent their pictures. Equally unfortunately, neither of us kept detailed records of where the photos had come from. For that reason I have listed photos I am unable to attribute as being part of the Down Collection. Where possible, I have given the name of the photographer and/or the donor. If I have slighted anyone, I apologize now. It certainly is not my intention to neglect giving credit where credit is due.

I wish to thank the following people for their kindness and support in this project: to Richard Provenzano for pushing me to do it; to Stephen Carlson for his advice and for access to his collection; to my aunt, Phyllis Spidell, for the use of the family albums and for the wonderful oral history of our family she has passed on to me over the years; to my sisters, Susan Down, Ellen Down, and Luanne Blanchard, for their forbearance as I tried to settle our father's estate and produce the book at the same time; and to photographer Frank Bond, who gave me photographs from his files and made me a print of the Civil War monitor USS *Saugus*.

Finally, I want to thank my wonderful wife Maureen—who suffered the messy house, the temper flare-ups, the long-delayed home projects, and many other trials and tribulations at my hands—all my love.

Norman Down

Introduction

This book is intended to be an extension of the work started with the late Helen Cutter of Saugus. It will focus on the development of the town between the years of approximately 1890–1965. I wish to show Saugus' progression from a rural farming community to its more recent role as a bustling suburb of Boston. This includes the development of a modest amount of industry, a middle-class residential community, and the effects of having a major highway pass through the middle of the town.

The photographs were gathered from a wide variety of sources, including family albums, postcards, and files of a professional photographer, as well as those of amateur photographers. Several institutions were also extremely helpful. They include Saugus Historical Society, Saugus Public Library, Lynn Historical Society, Lynn Public Library, and the Essex Institute of Salem.

Like all communities, Saugus is unique. Saugus traces its history from the earliest colonial period and was the site of America's first successful ironworks. A Saugus citizen played an important role in the purchase of Alaska from Imperial Russia. The town sent the largest contingent of Minutemen to fight at the Battle of Lexington and was also the site of one of the nation's first drive-in theaters. We have a pirate legend, and we have U.S. Navy vessels named for our town. We have produced coffee, chocolate, tobacco, and milled goods. We have also produced a number of scoundrels, scalawags, and eccentrics, as well as a Congressional Medal of Honor winner and a president of Harvard College.

America's first highway passes through Saugus and in the process has changed the town's nature dramatically. New England's first air-mail flight took off from a Saugus marsh. There is even a community in California named for our town.

It is my intention to show a limited slice of this town's rich history. In this respect, I have concentrated largely on that which no longer exists. I couldn't possibly include everything of interest, so I have not tried to. Although my history of Saugus is limited in scope, I hope that you enjoy it.

One

Buildings and Neighborhoods

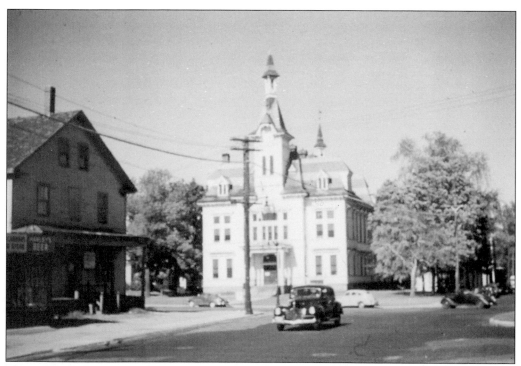

This is Saugus Center in the summer of 1948. At the left is Tilden's Store (the original Third Parish Meeting House). Saugus was still a small, almost rural, town. (Photograph courtesy of Sidney Smith.)

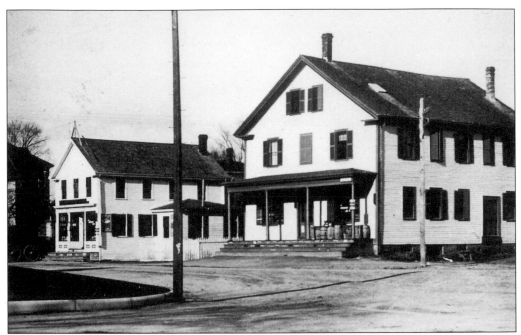

These two buildings stood on Main Street in Saugus Center, where the liquor store and the Gulf station are now located. The building at the left was a hardware store. (Photograph courtesy of the Down Collection.)

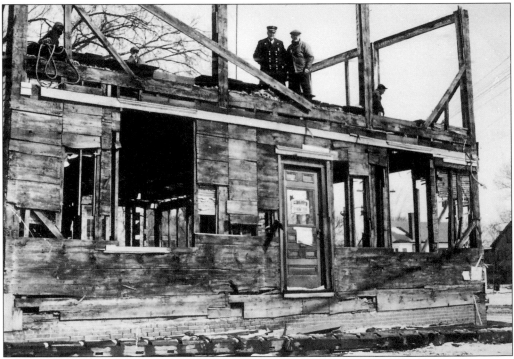

The Third Parish Meeting House was dismantled in the late 1940s. The man on the left is Fire Chief George Drew. On the right is William Stewart Oliver. (Photograph courtesy of the Down Collection.)

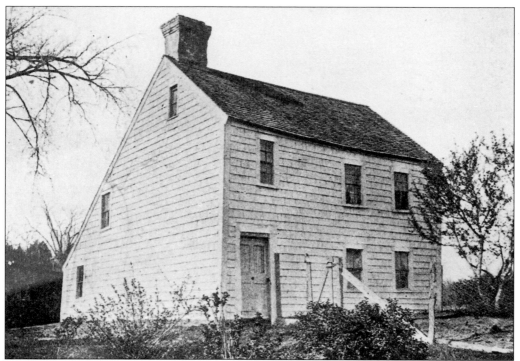

The Samuel Boardman House was located opposite the Bennett Boardman House on Howard Street in Oaklandvale. It was then the oldest house in town. (Photograph courtesy of the Provenzano Collection.)

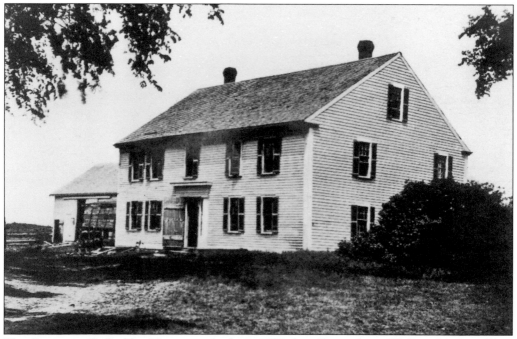

The Benjamin B. Raddin House was built in 1770. It still stands on Walnut Street, a short distance from the old North Saugus School. (Photograph courtesy of the Down Collection.)

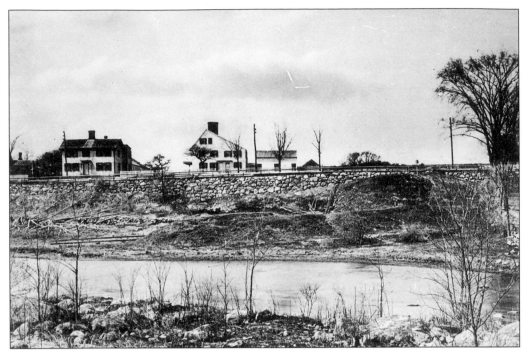

This is the Iron Works site in the early 1900s, before any restoration work was done. Central Street ran along the fence at the top of the stone wall. (Photograph courtesy of George Bliss, Carlson Collection)

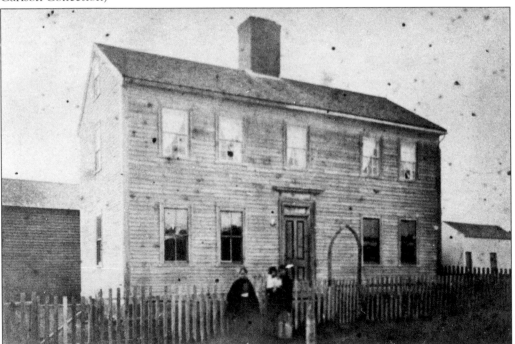

The Mansfield House was on Central Street, next to the Ironmaster's home. The Mansfield family produced two Saugus police chiefs, Roland Sr. and Roland Jr. (Photograph courtesy of the Carlson Collection.)

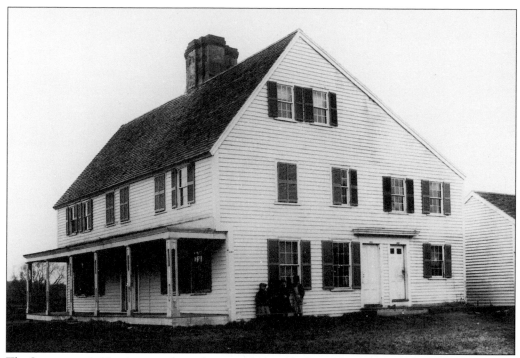

The Ironmaster's House went through many changes before it was restored by Wallace Nutting. This is how it looked around 1900. (Photograph courtesy of the Carlson Collection.)

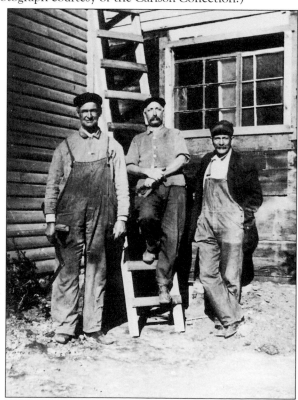

In this photograph, workmen take a break during the restoration in 1916. (Photograph courtesy of the Carlson Collection.)

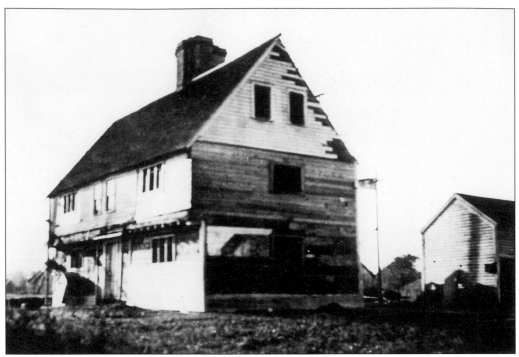

This is a photograph of the Ironmaster's House during restoration. Nutting researched similar houses in England for details. In the process of removing the front wall sheathing, it was discovered that the house had originally had a projecting upper story. (Photograph courtesy of the Carlson Collection.)

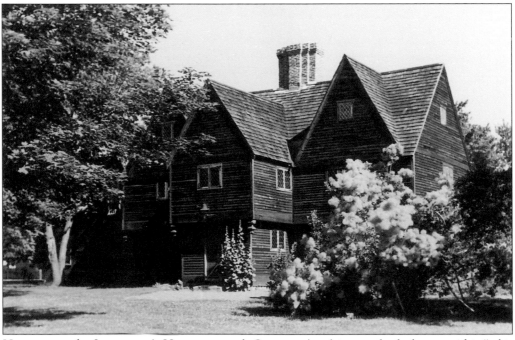

Here we see the Ironmaster's House restored. One noted architectural scholar termed it "a bit fanciful." (Photograph courtesy of the Carlson Collection.)

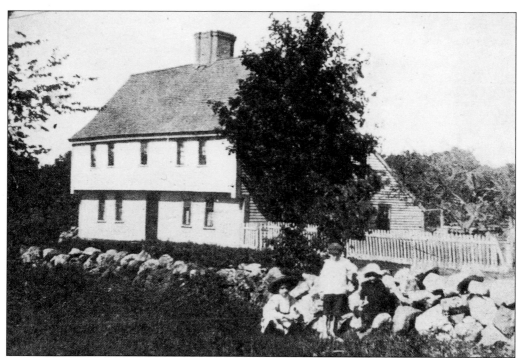

This is the Bennett-Boardman House in Oaklandvale. The house has never been moved but, because of changing boundaries, has been located in Essex and Suffolk Counties and also in the communities of Boston, Chelsea, Lynn, and Saugus. (Photograph courtesy of the Down Collection.)

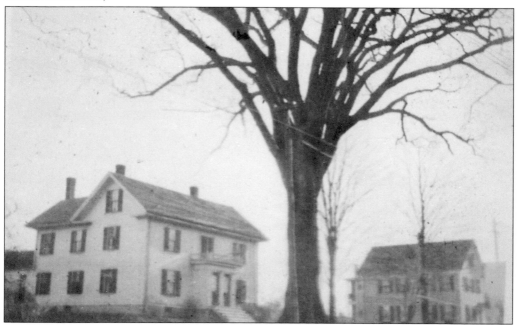

The Roby Elm was planted by Parson Roby in front of his house on Main Street. Because of the Dutch Elm Disease, it was taken down on November 6, 1951. (Photograph courtesy of the Down Collection.)

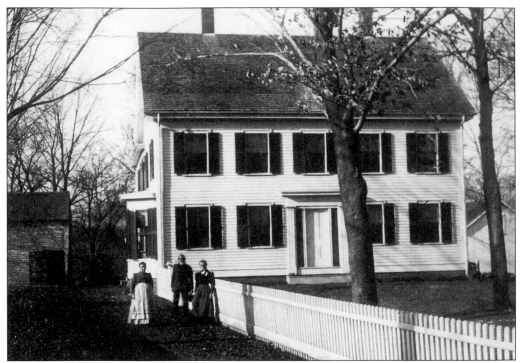

The Samuel Hawkes House was built by his father, Ahijah Hawkes, around 1800. It stood on what is the now the parking lot of the Saugus Plaza, at the corner of Walnut Street and Route One. (Photograph courtesy of the Down Collection.)

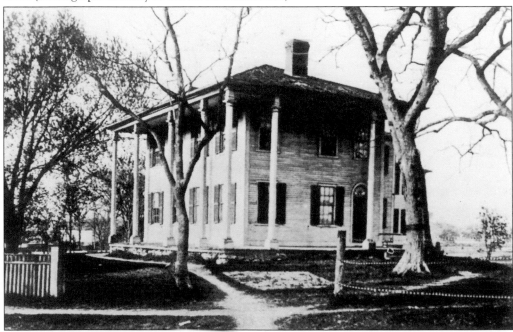

This house was built sometime in the early 1800s by Dr. Abijah Cheever, a surgeon in the Revolutionary War. The home still stands at 221 Essex Street. (Photograph courtesy of the Down Collection.)

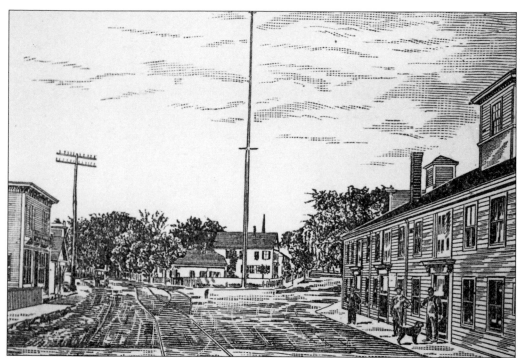

This is Franklin Square in East Saugus. On the left is Lincoln Avenue, and on the right is Chestnut Street, c. 1900. (Photograph courtesy of the Down Collection.)

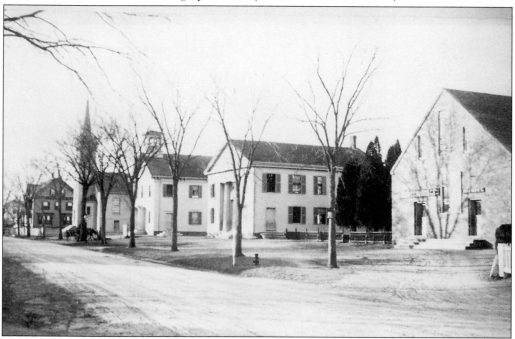

This is Main Street, Saugus Center, c. 1880. The building second from the right was the original town hall. It was later moved behind the school (third from right) where it became the American Legion Hall. The Roby School was built in the town hall's place on Main Street in 1895. (Photograph courtesy of the Down Collection.)

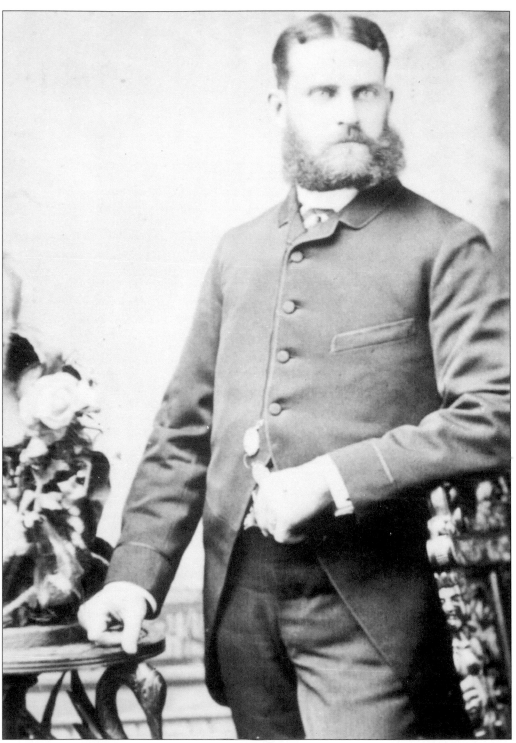

Mr. Smith, who developed the residential area known as Sweetser's Corner into the commercial area now called Cliftondale Square, was the son-in-law of Charles Augustus Sweetser. (Photograph courtesy of the Down Collection.)

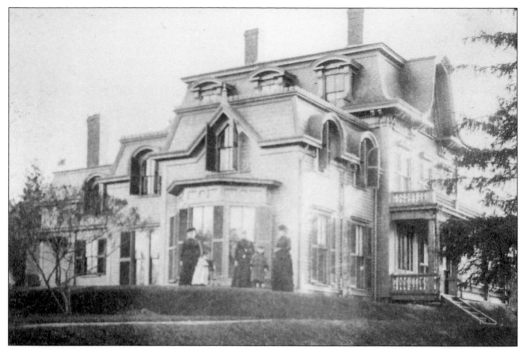

"Grassmount," the estate built by Charles Augustus Sweetser in 1866, stood on the corner of Lincoln Avenue and Smith Road. Sweetser's son-in-law, Mr. Smith, later lived in the house. (Photograph courtesy of the Down Collection.)

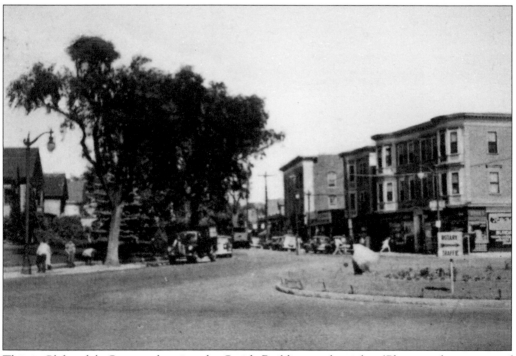

This is Cliftondale Square, showing the Smith Building at the right. (Photograph courtesy of the Down Collection.)

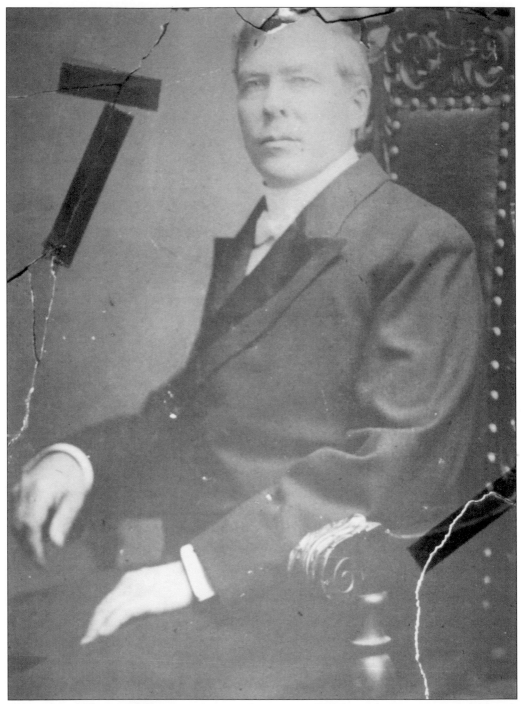

This is Rev. Norman McKinnon, who served as pastor of Cliftondale Congregational Church from June 4, 1905, to October 20 1907. (Photograph from the files of the Congregational Church, Down Collection.)

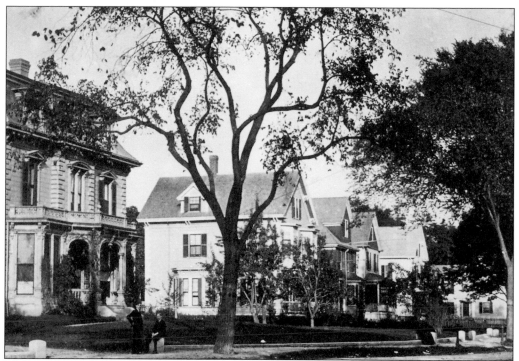

Here we see Lincoln Avenue, Cliftondale, looking toward Lynn. The Bond Mansion is on the left and is situated on the corner of Lincoln Avenue and Jackson Street. (Photograph courtesy of the Down Collection.)

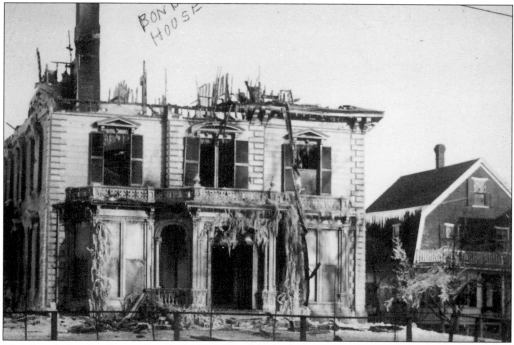

The Bond Mansion burned around 1915. The Methodists, who had recently lost their church to fire, built a new church on this site. (Photograph courtesy of the Down Collection.)

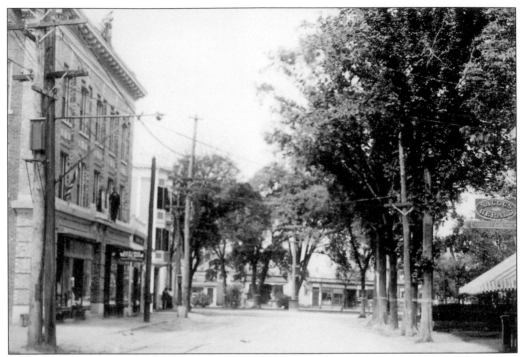

This is Lincoln Avenue, looking into Cliftondale Square from the Lynn side. The Odd Fellows Building at left was burned around 1950. As a result, the third floor was removed. (Photograph courtesy of the Down Collection.)

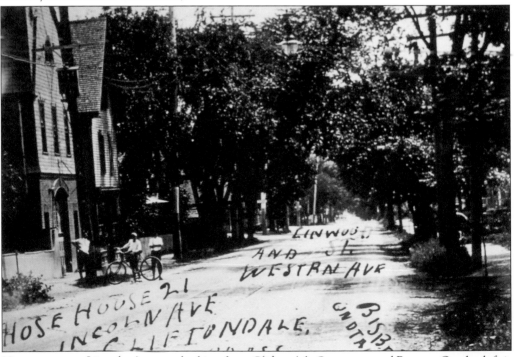

Here we are on Lincoln Avenue, looking from Cliftondale Square toward Revere. On the left is the Cliftondale Fire House. (Photograph courtesy of the Down Collection.)

22

Two

Men in Uniform:
Police, Fire,
and Military

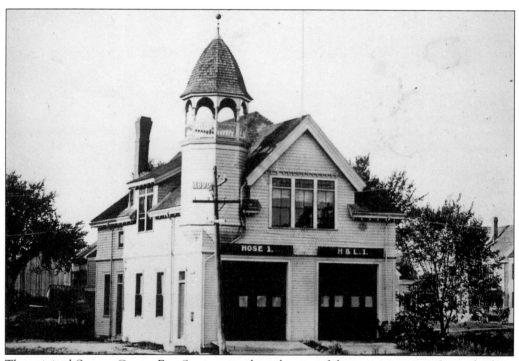

The original Saugus Center Fire Station stood on the site of the present station. It was built in 1891 and originally had only one door. The door on the right was added when the town bought a second truck. (Photograph courtesy of the Down Collection.)

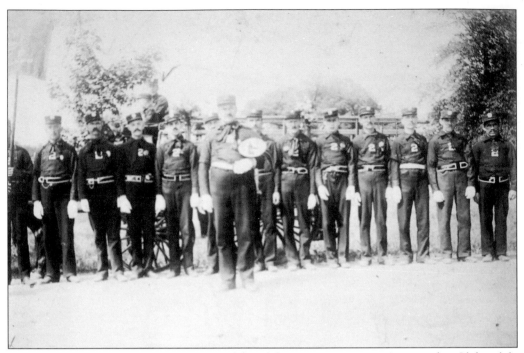

Here we see Saugus Fire Department Cliftondale Hose Company #2, near the Cliftondale station in the early 1880s. (Photograph courtesy of the Down Collection.)

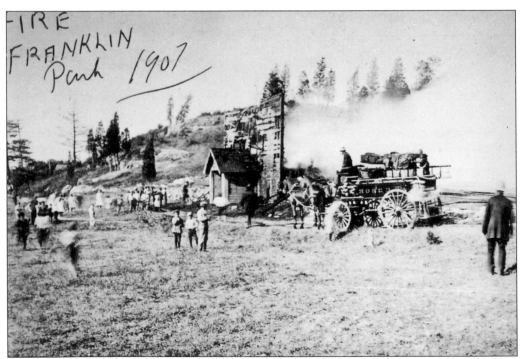

A barn was destroyed by fire at the Parsons' farm at Franklin Park, near the Revere line. The Cliftondale Hose Company responded but was able to save very little. (Photograph courtesy of the Down Collection.)

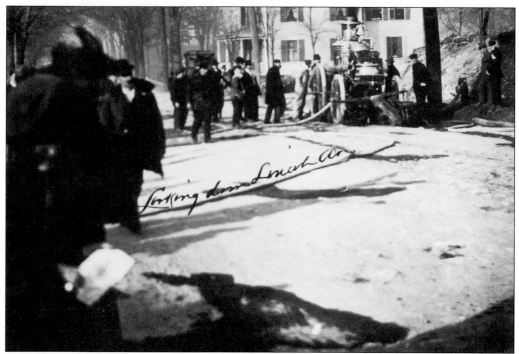

This fire took place in the vicinity of Clifton Avenue on April 8, 1908. Several houses and barns were destroyed in this blaze. (Photograph courtesy of the Down Collection.)

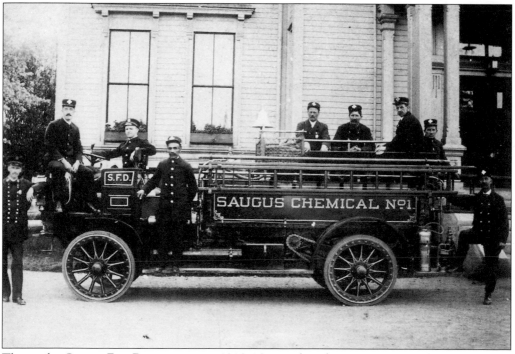

This is the Saugus Fire Department, c. 1910. Notice that there is pavement directly in front of town hall, instead of several yards away, as it is currently. (Photograph courtesy of the Down Collection.)

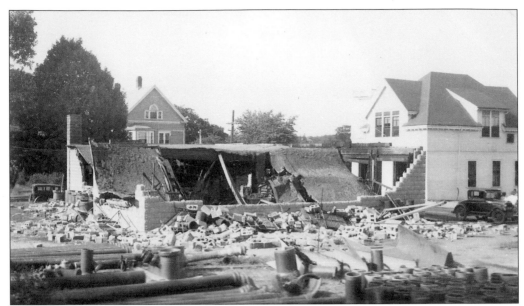

An explosion and fire destroyed the old Public Works garage on Hamilton Street in 1933. Fire Chief Mellon Joy died fighting this terrible blaze. (Photograph courtesy of Phyllis Spidell, Down Collection.)

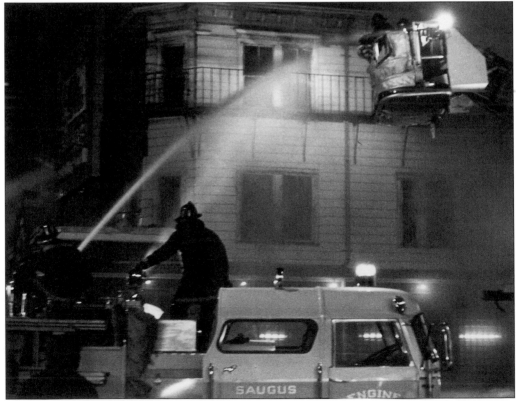

Here, Saugus firefighters are fighting a blaze in the1950s. Unfortunately, the date and location of the photograph are unknown. (Photograph courtesy of Paul Carlson, Carlson Collection.)

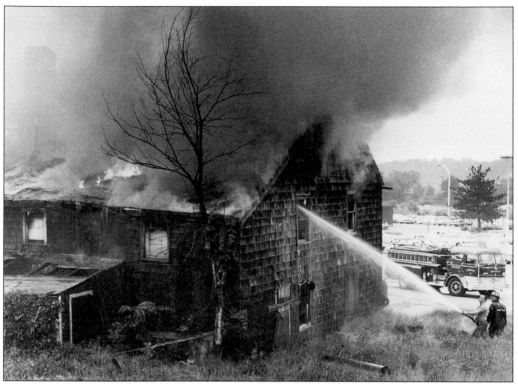

Fire destroys one of the old Hawkes houses in Oaklandvale. It was located behind what is now Russo's Candy Shop. (Photograph courtesy of Paul Carlson, Carlson Collection.)

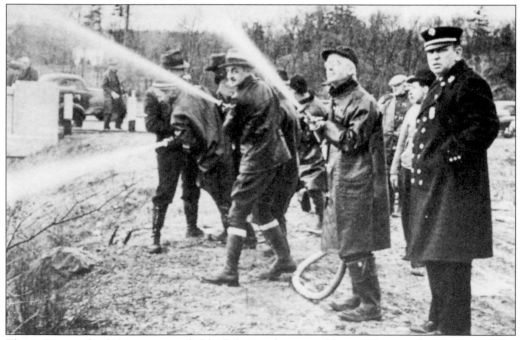

These Saugus firefighters are probably fighting the same blaze. (Photograph courtesy of the Carlson Collection.)

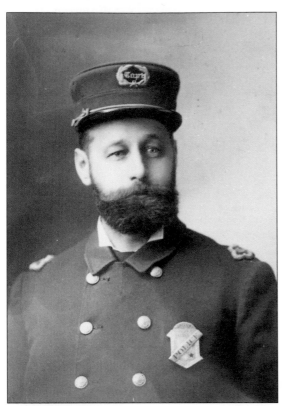

This is a picture of Captain (later Chief) Roland L. Mansfield of the Saugus Police Department. (Photograph courtesy of Leona Mansfield Cutter, Carlson Collection.)

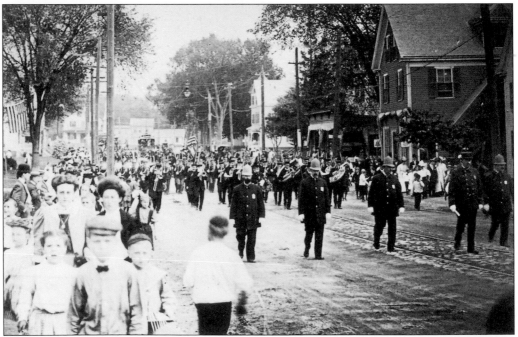

Chief Roland Mansfield leads the Saugus Police Department in a GAR parade on May 30, year unknown. They are on Central Street passing the corner of Jasper Street. (Photograph courtesy of the Down Collection.)

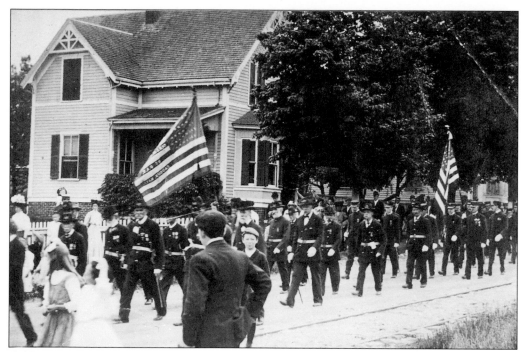

GAR veterans are marching in Saugus Center, on Winter Street, c. 1900. These Civil War veterans honored their fallen comrades every Memorial Day. (Photograph courtesy of the Down Collection.)

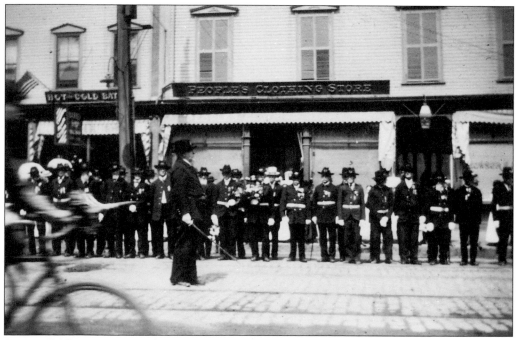

Saugus GAR veterans stand at attention at a parade, probably in Lynn. (Photograph courtesy of the Down Collection.)

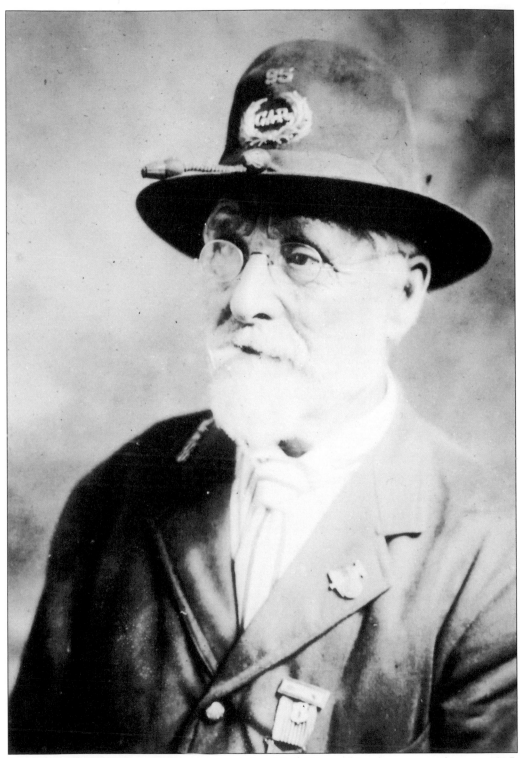

Samuel L. Blood was a GAR veteran of the Civil War. This photo was taken c. 1915. (Photograph courtesy of the Provenzano Collection.)

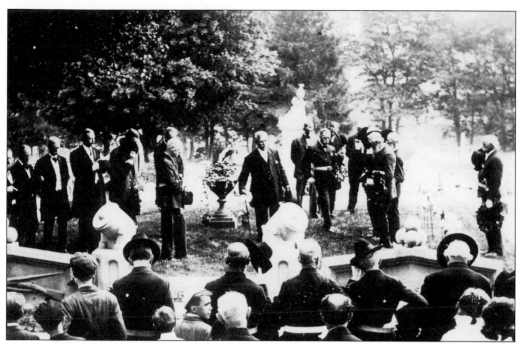

Memorial Day ceremonies at Riverside Cemetery always included patriotic speeches to honor the veterans' fallen comrades. (Photograph courtesy of the Down Collection.)

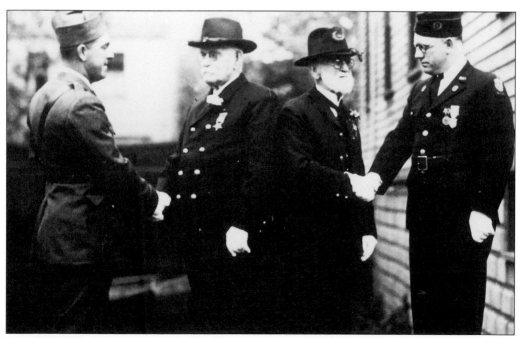

In this May 30, 1932 photograph, World War I veterans shake hands with GAR vets. From left to right are: Ted Jacquith, Joseph Newhall, Dr. George Gale, and Fred Hawkes. (Photograph courtesy of the Down Collection.)

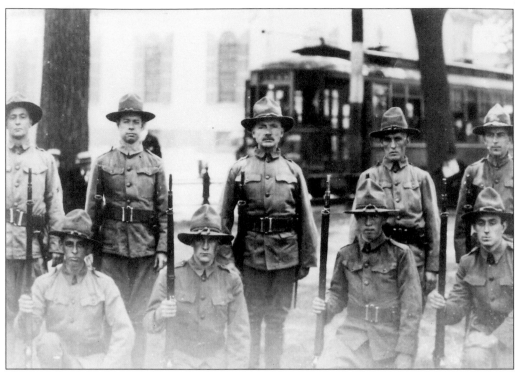

This is a detail of a photo marked, "12th Regiment of Mass. State Guard—Saugus, Massachusetts, May 30, 1919." (Photograph courtesy of the Down Collection.)

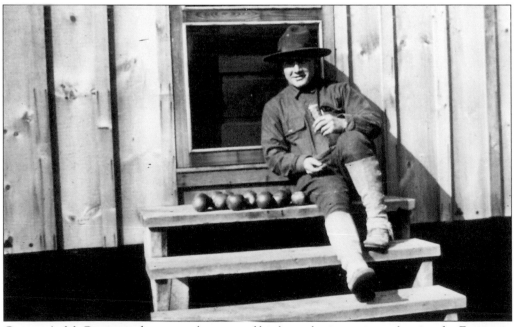

George A. McCarrier is shown on the steps of his barracks, just prior to leaving for Europe in World War I. (Photograph courtesy of the McCarrier Family, Down Collection.)

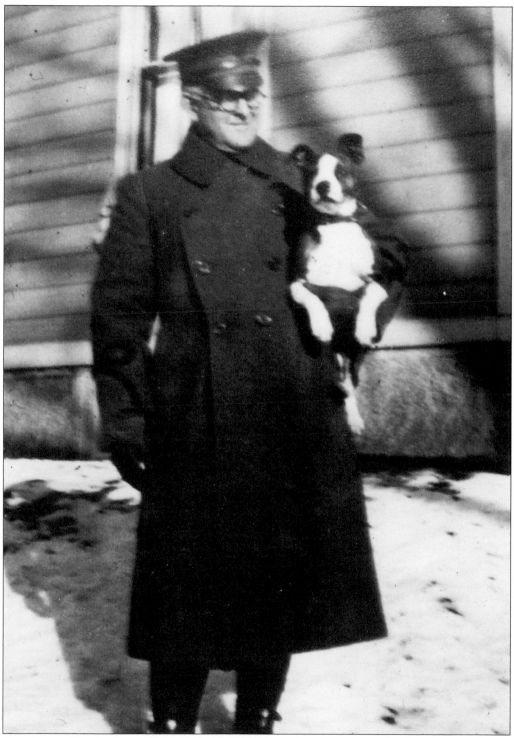

Dr. George C. Parcher, noted Saugus physician and surgeon, was the first Saugus doctor to report for service in World War I. He died in August 1917. (Photograph courtesy of the Down Collection.)

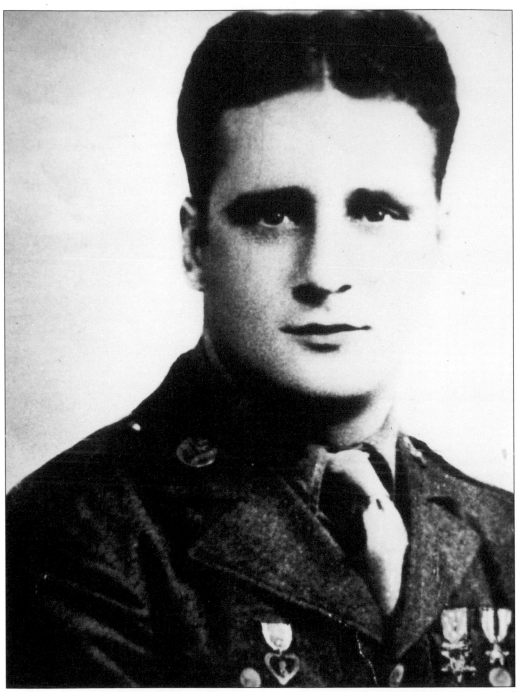

Staff Sgt. Arthur F. DeFranzo was killed in action in France in 1944. He repeatedly attacked an enemy machine-gun nest single-handedly to protect his men. For his heroism, he was posthumously awarded the Congressional Medal of Honor. (Photograph courtesy of Lee Marino, Down Collection.)

Three

Churches

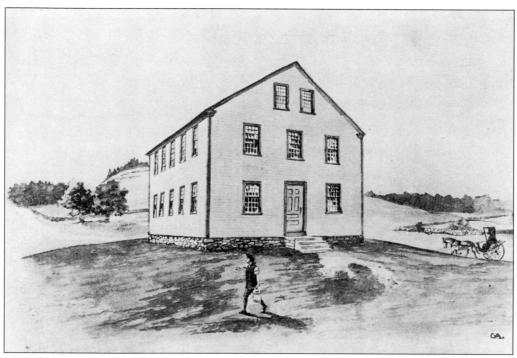

The Third Parish Meeting House was located where the Civil War monument now stands in Saugus Center. (Photograph courtesy of the Down Collection.)

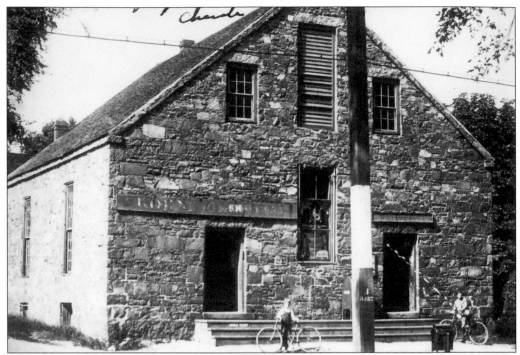

The "Park Press Building" was constructed in 1835 as a Unitarian church. In this view, we see it as a store (on the left) and a post office (on the right), c.1890. (Photograph courtesy of the Down Collection.)

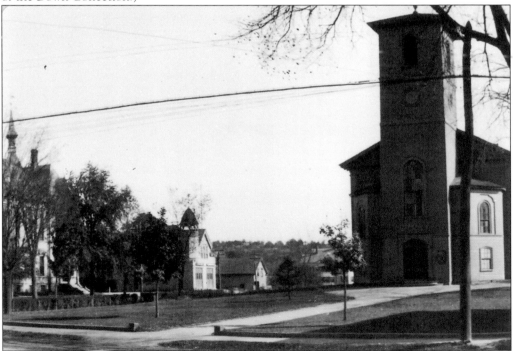

At the right is the Saugus Center Congregational Church. The building with the tower, at left, was the fire station. (Photograph courtesy of the Down Collection.)

The Union Church on Walnut Street in North Saugus is shown under construction, c. 1870. (Photograph courtesy of the Down Collection.)

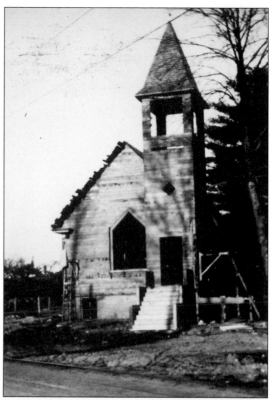

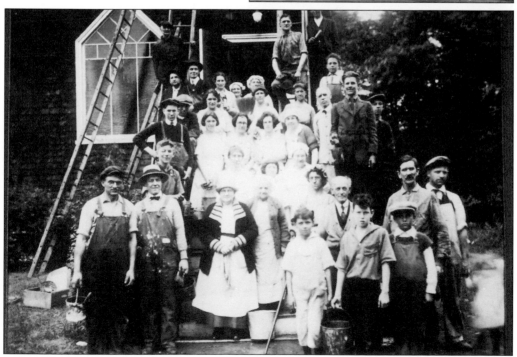

It's paint-up and clean-up day at the Union Church in 1921. (Photograph courtesy of the Down Collection.)

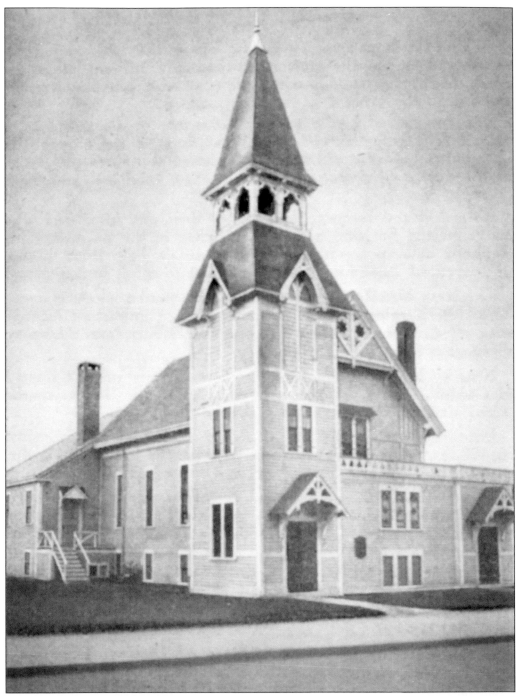

The original Cliftondale Methodist Church was located at 493 Lincoln Avenue, diagonally across the street from the present post office. (Photograph courtesy of the Down Collection.)

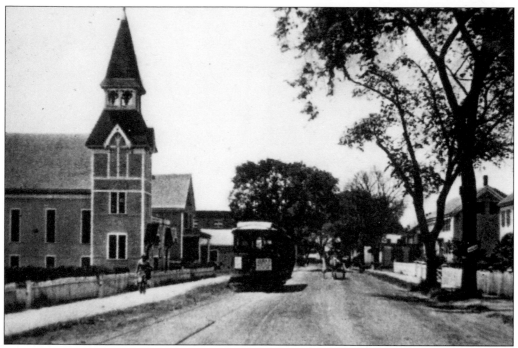

This is a postcard view looking west down Lincoln Avenue in Cliftondale. In a modern picture, the post office would be at the right. (Photograph courtesy of the Down Collection.)

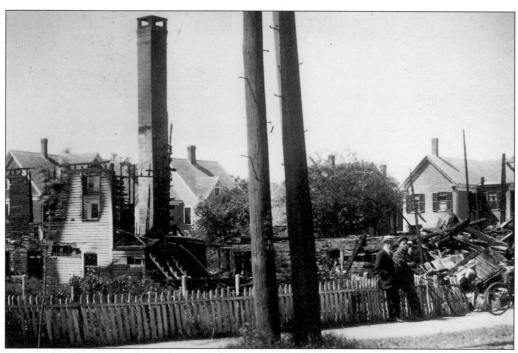

This is the aftermath of the fire that destroyed the Cliftondale Methodist Church in 1914. (Photograph courtesy of the Down Collection.)

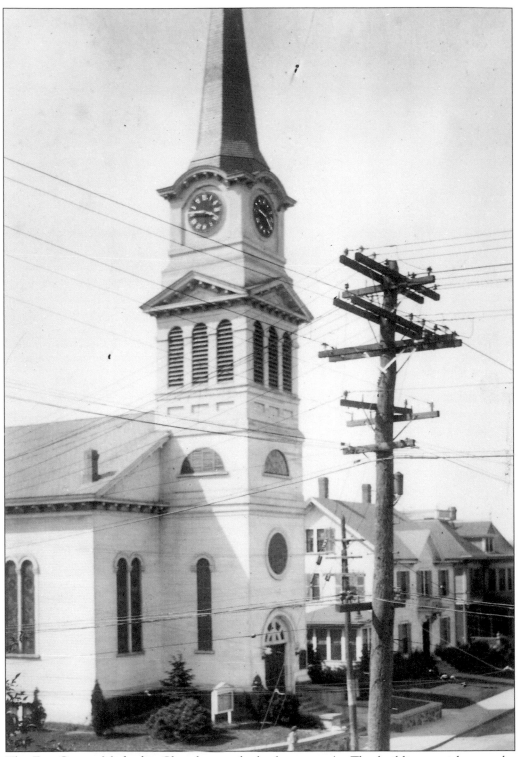

The East Saugus Methodist Church once had a huge steeple. The building at right was the Saugus General Hospital. (Photograph courtesy of the Carlson Collection.)

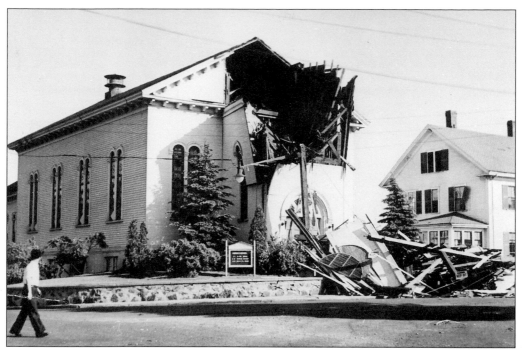

The church's steeple toppled during a violent storm. (Photograph courtesy of Paul R. Carlson, Carlson Collection.)

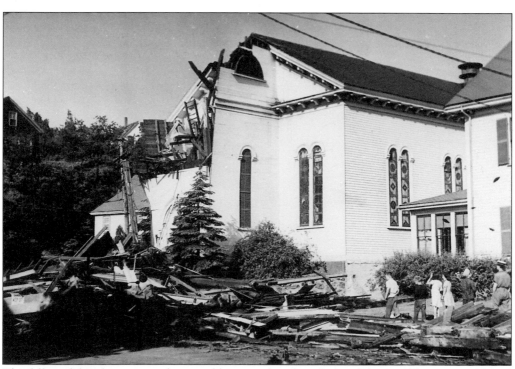

The falling debris here narrowly missed hitting a boy from Lynn. (Photograph courtesy of Paul R. Carlson, Carlson Collection.)

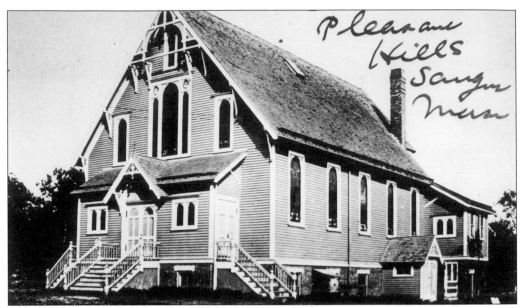

The original Blessed Sacrament Church was located on Adams Avenue. Later, a single-story church was built on the corner of Churchill Street and Central Street. This photo was taken c. 1900. (Photograph courtesy of the Down Collection.)

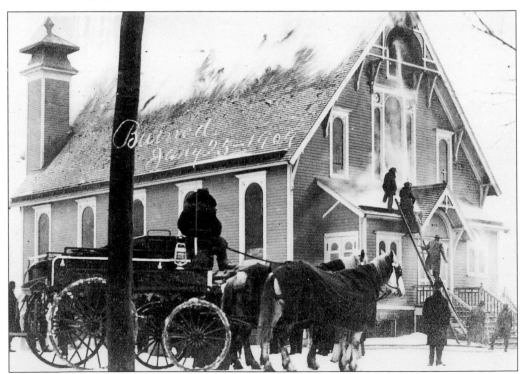

The church was destroyed by fire on January 25, 1904. Note the blankets on the horses. The animals would get sweaty pulling the fire wagon and then would have to stand for hours in the freezing cold. (Photograph courtesy of the Down Collection.)

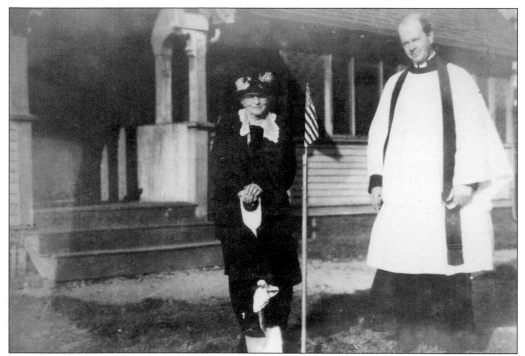

Mrs. Ashworth donated the money for an addition to St. John's Episcopal Church in Saugus Center. Here, we see her at the ground-breaking ceremony. (Photograph courtesy of the Down Collection.)

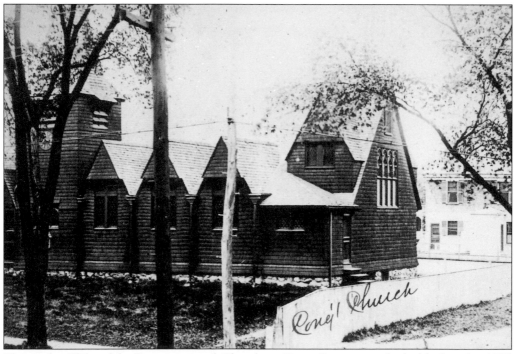

This is the Cliftondale Congregational Church on Essex Street, as it looked before the 1935 fire. (Photograph courtesy of the Down Collection.)

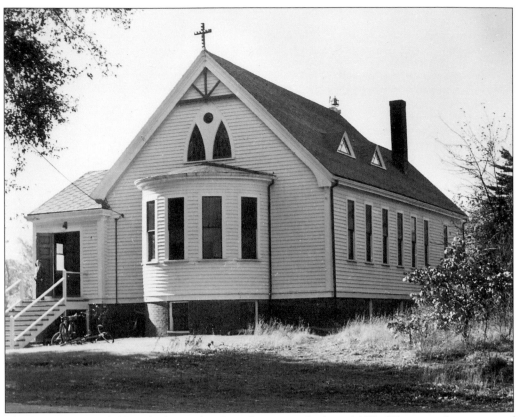

The Dorr Memorial Church, located in Lynnhurst, was built in 1877. (Photograph courtesy of Frank Bond.)

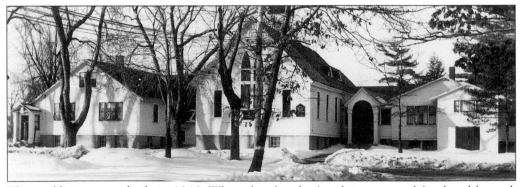

These additions were built in 1946. When the church closed, it was vandalized and burned. (Photograph courtesy of Frank Bond.)

Four

Stores, Industries, and Businesses

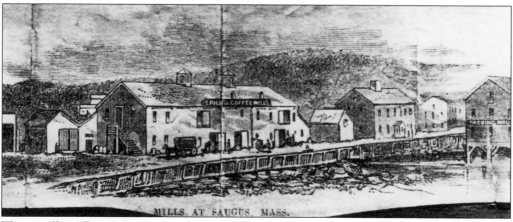

These mills in East Saugus ground tobacco, grain, and chocolate at various times. They were operated by the movement of the tides in and out of the Saugus River. This picture is c. 1800. (Photograph courtesy of the Down Collection.)

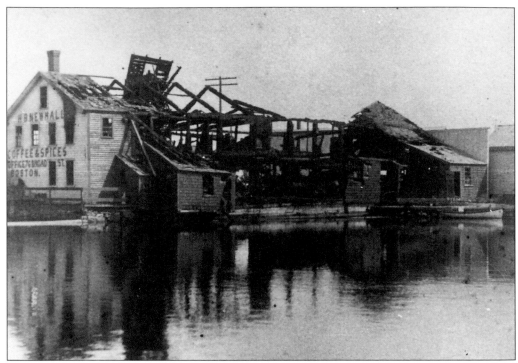

Newhall's mill was destroyed by fire in 1907. Ironically, the East Saugus fire station was directly across the street. (Photograph courtesy of the Down Collection.)

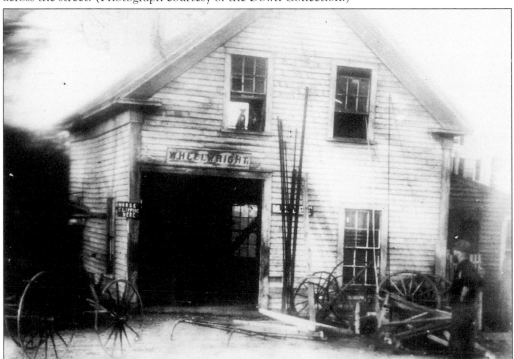

Ward's Blacksmith Shop was located on Hamilton Street, next to the fire station. (Photograph courtesy of the Carlson Collection.)

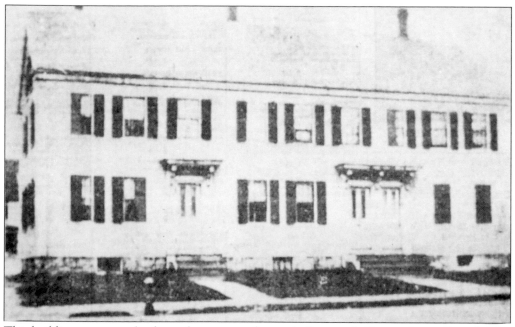

This building was once the first tobacco manufactory in Sweetser's Corner. It stood on the site of the present Surabian Building. (Photograph courtesy of the Down Collection.)

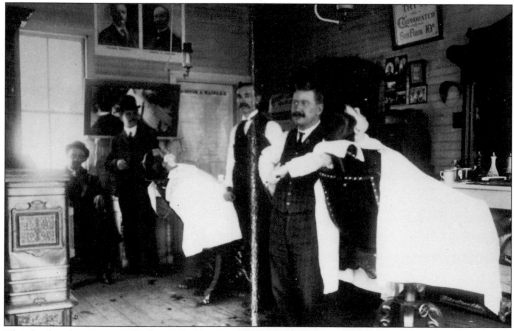

This barbershop was in Cliftondale Square. Note the pictures of President Theodore Roosevelt and his running mate, Charles W. Fairbanks. (Photograph courtesy of the Down Collection.)

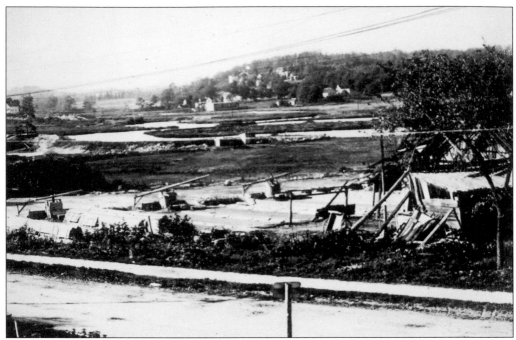

The Stocker Brickyard was located between Winter Street and the Saugus River. Several locations in Saugus had good quality clay; some of it was used for making dishes. (Photograph courtesy of the Down Collection.)

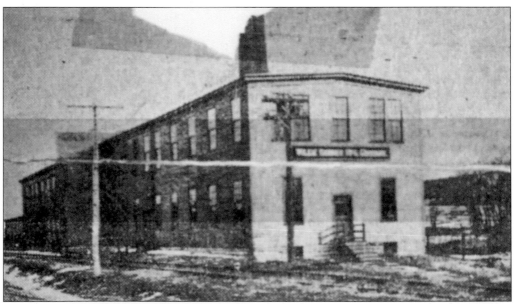

This is one of the many factories that were once situated along the Saugus branch of the B & M Railroad. This one was located between Saugus Center and East Saugus. (Photograph courtesy of the Down Collection.)

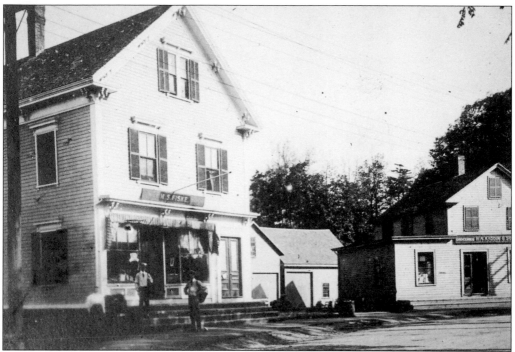

Here are Fiske's Store and Raddin's Store on Jackson Street, *c.* 1900. Fiske's Store was later torn down, and the building housing George's Barber Shop replaced it. (Photograph courtesy of the Down Collection.)

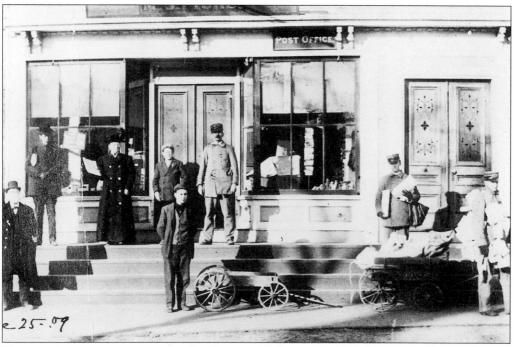

These mailmen are preparing to make Christmas deliveries in 1909. The post office was located in Fiske's Store at the time. (Photograph courtesy of the Provenzano Collection.)

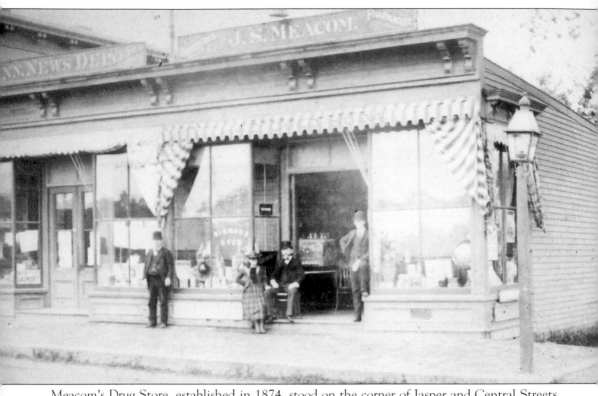

Meacom's Drug Store, established in 1874, stood on the corner of Jasper and Central Streets. From left to right are: Mr. Dunne, Mable Hill, Mr. Meacom, and Will (last name unknown). (Photograph courtesy of the Down Collection.)

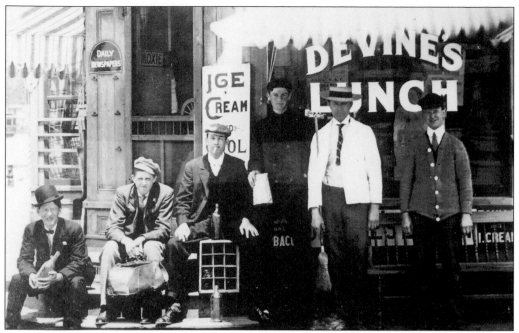

Devine's Lunch, later known as the State Luncheonette, was located near the railroad tracks and Central Street. The building is a sub shop today. (Photograph courtesy of the Down Collection.)

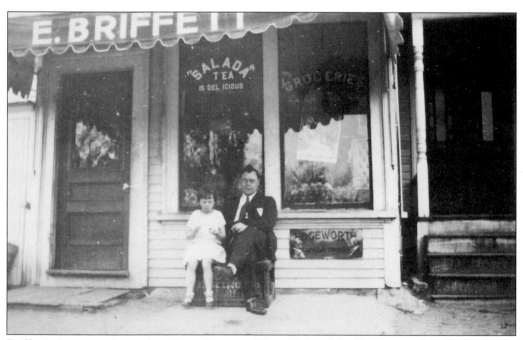

Briffett's Store was located on Essex Street in West Cliftondale. Here we see Mr. Briffett and a young friend. (Photograph courtesy of the Down Collection.)

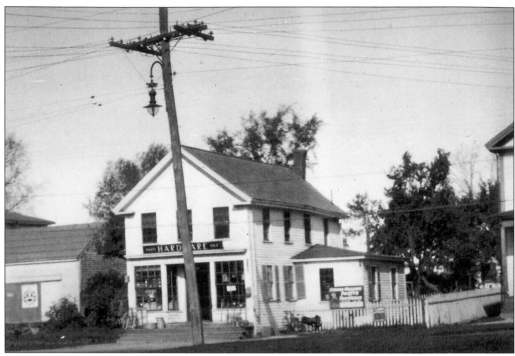

This hardware store was located at 7 Main Street. A liquor store now occupies this site. (Photograph courtesy of the Down Collection.)

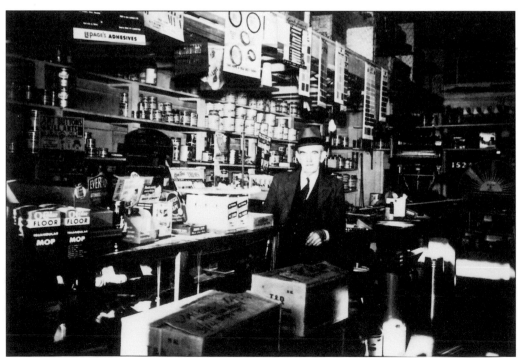

Mr. Adlington is shown here in his store in Saugus Center. His store was in the old Third Parish Meeting House. (Photograph courtesy of Iva Adlington, Down Collection.)

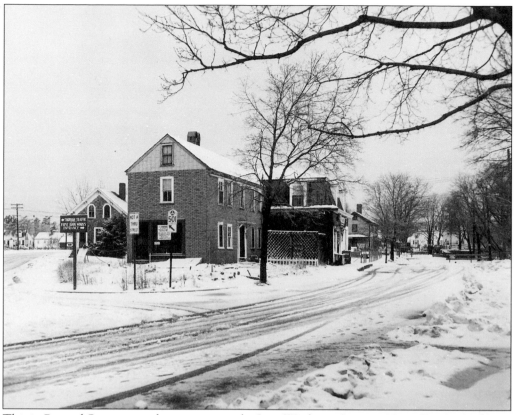

This is Central Street, near the entrance to the Iron Works, on January 22, 1953. The buildings closest to the camera have since been torn down. (Photograph courtesy of Richard Merrill, Iron Works Collection.)

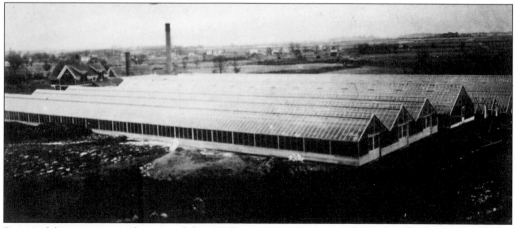

Pictured here are greenhouses of the William Sim Carnation Company, located on Morton Avenue. Sim created the basic red carnation that bears his name. (Photograph courtesy of the Down Collection.)

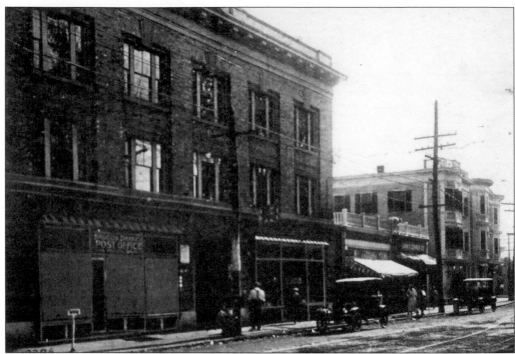

The Odd Fellows Building in Cliftondale Square housed the post office in the 1920s. Note that it had a third floor at that time. (Photograph courtesy of the Down Collection.)

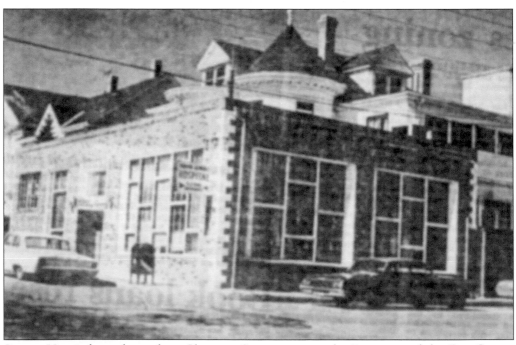

Saugus Hospital was located on Chestnut Street, next to the Parsonage of the East Saugus Methodist Church. The hospital closed in the 1970s and was torn down. (Photograph courtesy of the Down Collection.)

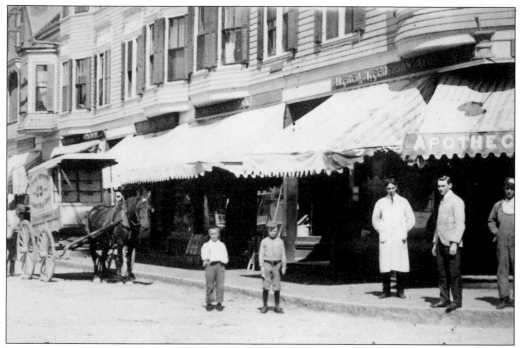

Ferguson's Apothecary (Butler Drug) was located on the corner of Jackson and Essex Streets in Cliftondale. The man in the long white coat is H. Warren Butler, who later bought the business. (Photograph courtesy of the Down Collection.)

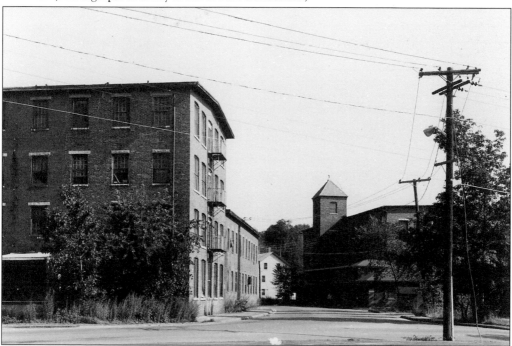

Pranker's Mill was located at the junction of Central and Elm Streets. The dam to power the mill created Pranker's Pond. This group of buildings is still in use. (Photograph courtesy of Paul R. Carlson, Carlson Collection.)

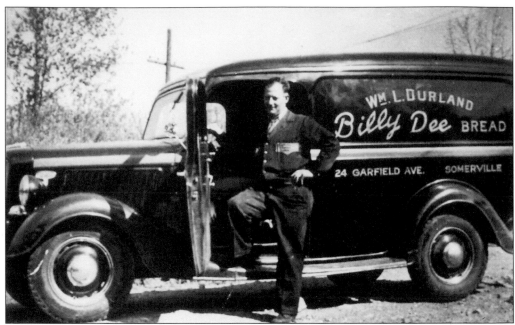

Bakery products were once sold door-to-door from bread trucks. Door-to-door selling and delivery were once very common. (Photograph courtesy of the Down Collection.)

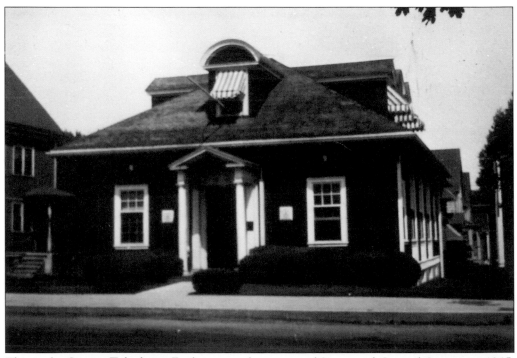

This is the Saugus Telephone Exchange at the corner of Stone and Central Streets, c. 1945. Each call was handled by an operator, and the telephone number consisted of four numbers and a letter (i.e. 1067J). (Photograph courtesy of the Down Collection.)

Five

That's Entertainment

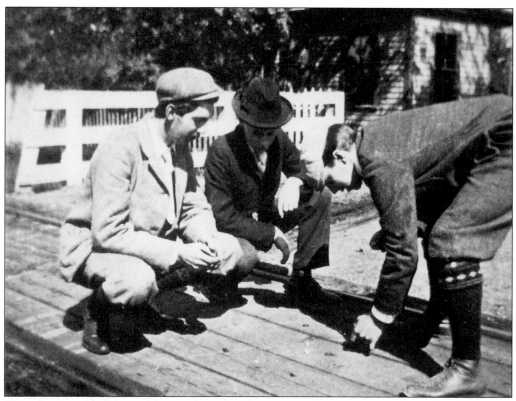

These boys are playing marbles on the railroad crossing on Essex Street in the early 1880s. From left to right are: Russell Clucas, unidentified, and Crawford Stocker Sr. Note the formal style of clothing. (Photograph courtesy of the Down Collection.)

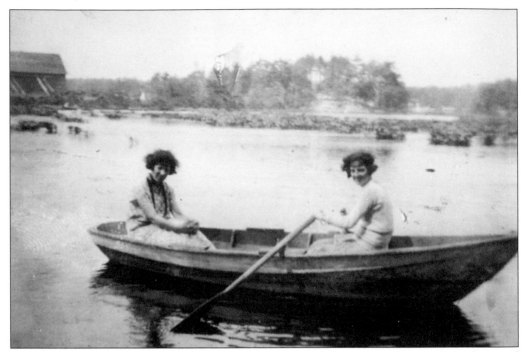

Boating on Pranker's Pond, later known as Lily Pond, was extremely popular. The pond developed as a recreation area and had its own refreshment stand. (Photograph courtesy of the Down Collection.)

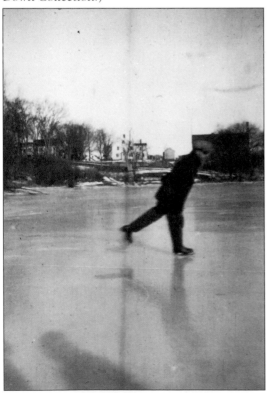

This is Percy Cutter skating on the Saugus River near the Iron Works. (Photograph courtesy of the Cutter Family, Down Collection.)

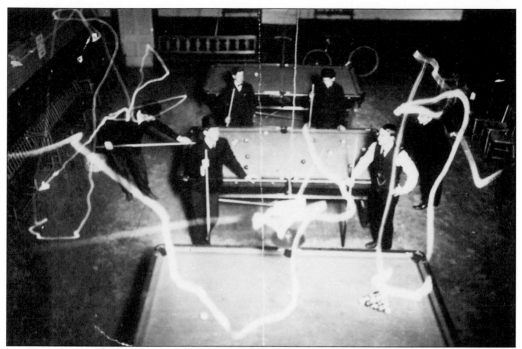

This pool hall was located on the second floor of the Cliftondale Fire Station. The cause of the light streaks is unknown. (Photograph courtesy of the Down Collection.)

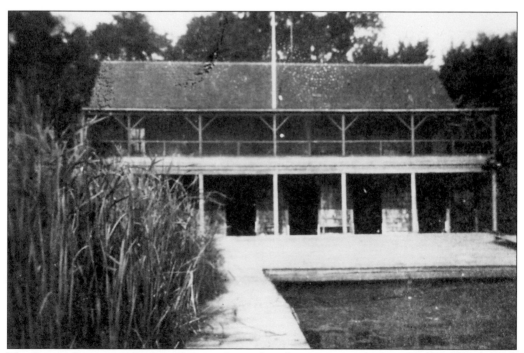

The Saugus Canoe and Tennis Club was located on the river, near the Iron Works. (Photograph courtesy of the Down Collection.)

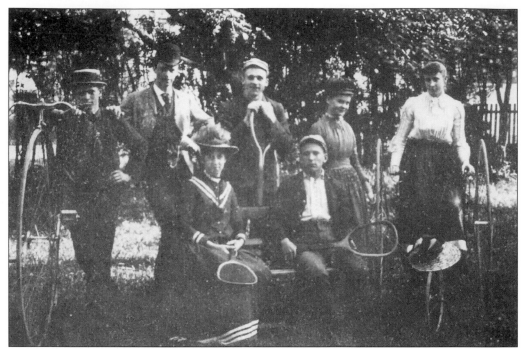

This is the Saugus Center Bicycle and Tennis Club, c. 1910. Note the high-wheeled bicycle and curved tennis racquets. (Photograph courtesy of the Down Collection.)

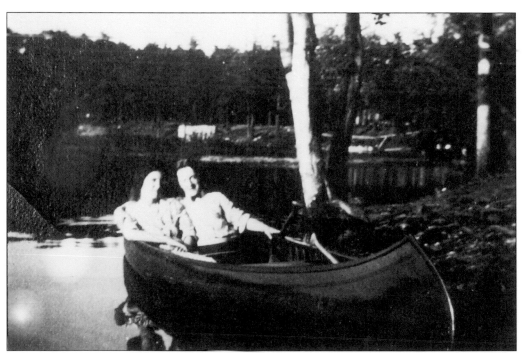

This couple is canoeing (canoodling?) on Lily Pond, c. 1940. (Photograph courtesy of the Down Collection.)

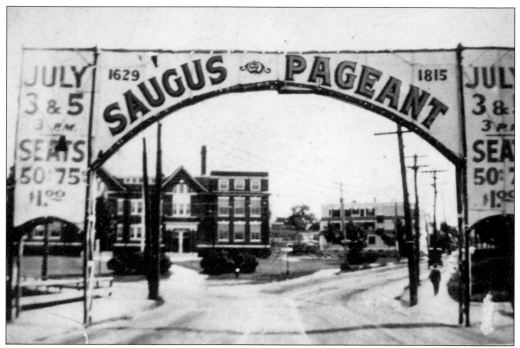

The Saugus Centennial Pageant celebrated the incorporation of Saugus as a town in 1815. (Photograph courtesy of the Provenzano Collection.)

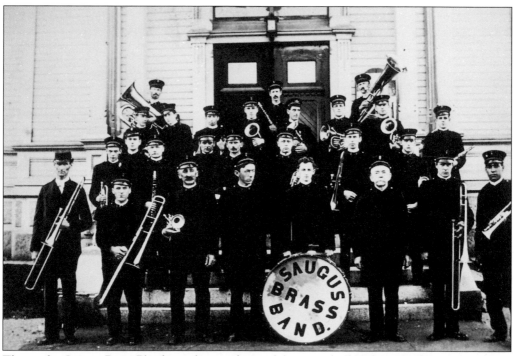

This is the Saugus Brass Band standing in front of the town hall. (Photograph courtesy of the Provenzano Collection.)

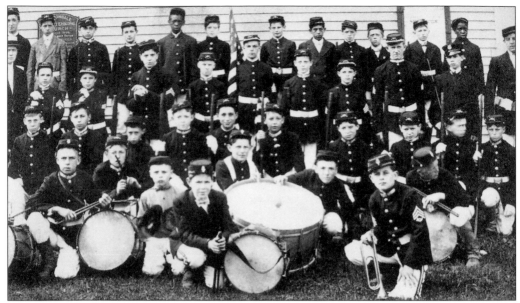

Rev. William M. Gilbert and his Boys Brigade Company K are shown here at the Cliftondale Methodist Church in 1910. (Photograph courtesy of the Down Collection.)

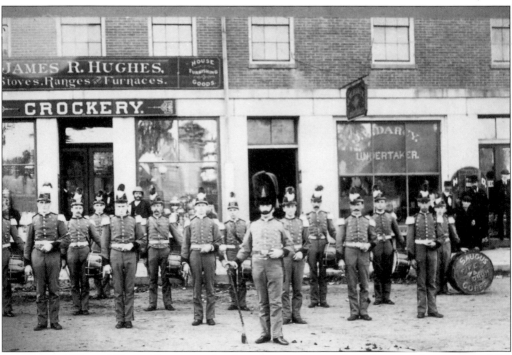

The Saugus Fife and Drum Corps pose for this picture at a parade. (Photograph courtesy of the Down Collection.)

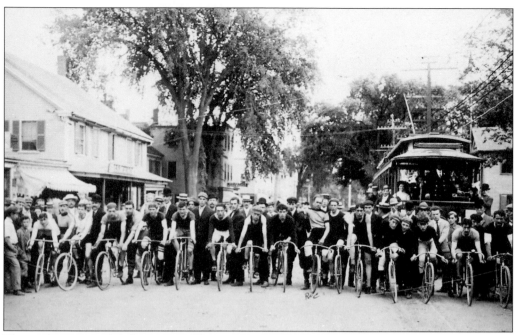

This is the racing club known as "The Wise Guys." Percy Cutter was a member. (Photograph courtesy of the Cutter Family, Down Collection.)

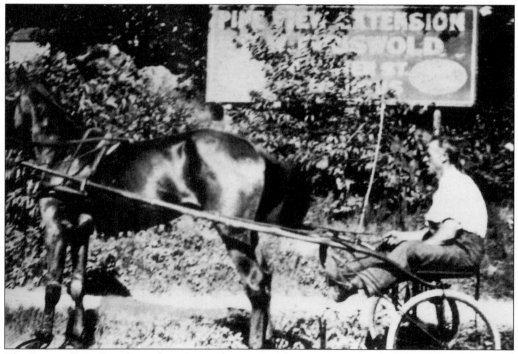

The Saugus Race Track on the salt marsh was used for trotting races. In later years, it was used for auto racing. (Photograph courtesy of Richard Provenzano, Down Collection.)

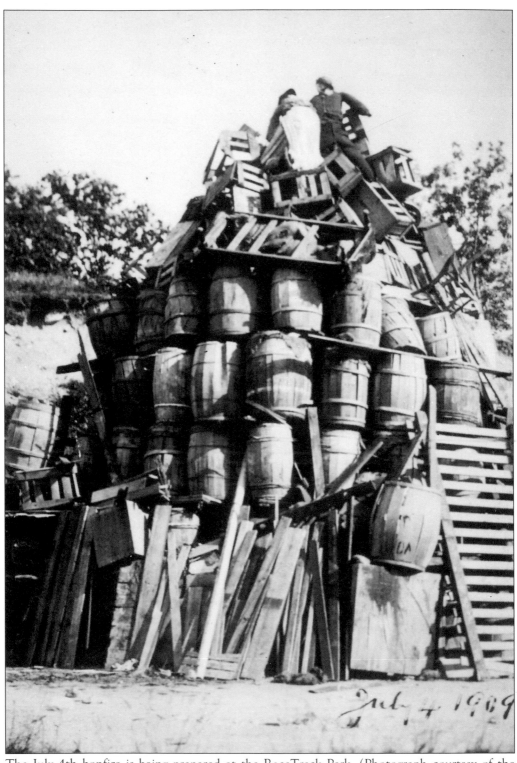

The July 4th bonfire is being prepared at the RaceTrack Park. (Photograph courtesy of the Down Collection.)

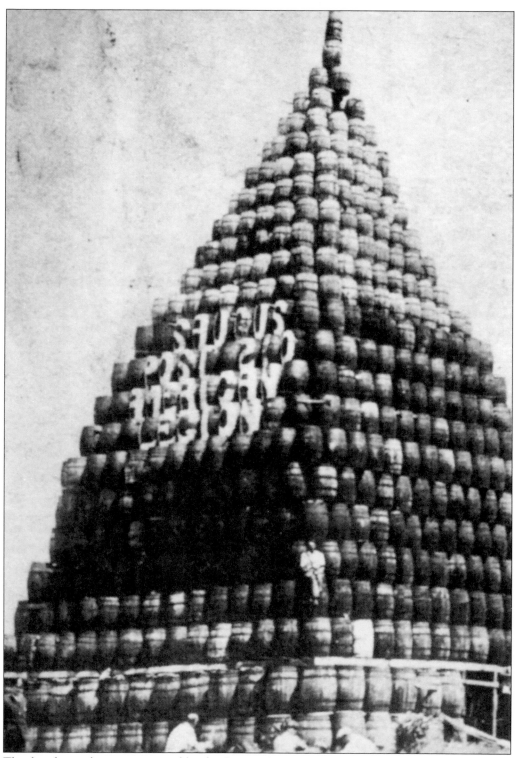

This bonfire-to-be was sponsored by the Saugus American Legion Post 210, as it was for many years. (Photograph courtesy of the Down Collection.)

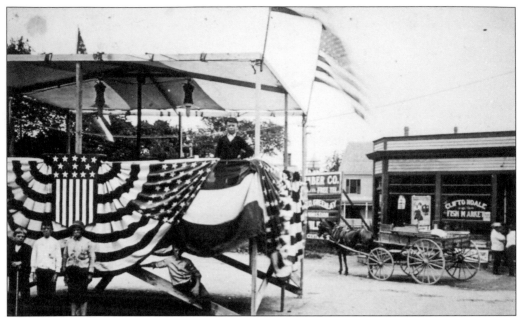

Here, Cliftondale Square is decorated for July 4, 1909. The background today is the Mobil station. (Photograph courtesy of the Down Collection.)

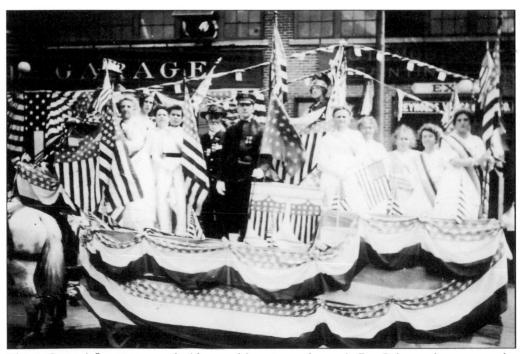

This is Saugus' float in a parade (date and location unknown). Dr. Gale can be seen on the float. (Photograph courtesy of the Down Collection.)

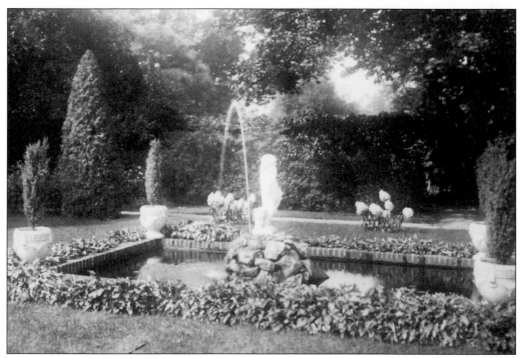

Peckham's sunken gardens were located at what was then 329 Central Street in Saugus Center. The same site today is the location of Hammersmith Apartments. (Photograph courtesy of the Down Collection.)

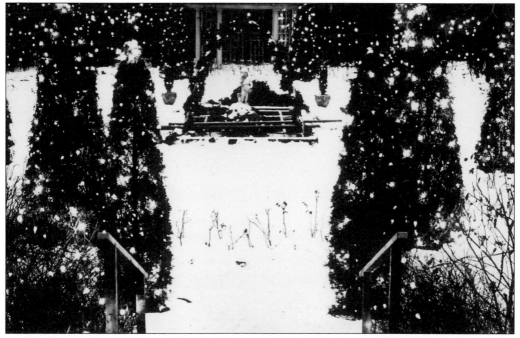

Peckham's gardens are decorated with Christmas lights. This was such a novelty in 1928, that it was necessary to put extra policemen on duty to handle the auto traffic from out-of-town visitors coming to see the spectacle. (Photograph courtesy of the Down Collection.)

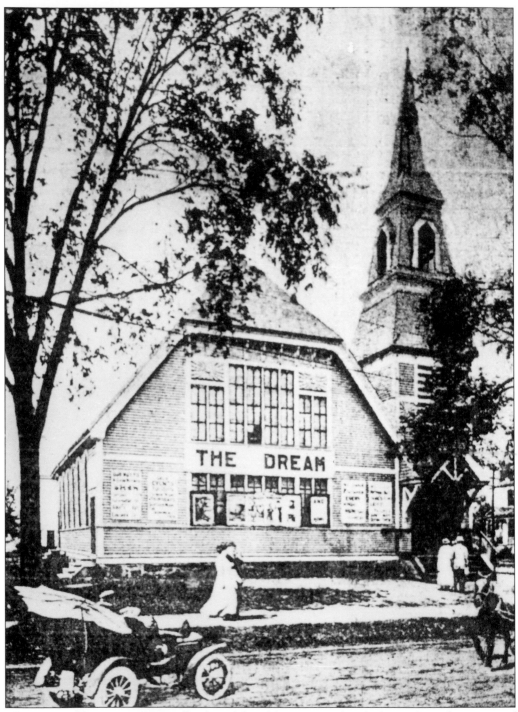

The Dream Theater was originally the Cliftondale Baptist Church, located on the corner of Essex and Mount Vernon Streets. When the theater burned in the late 1920s, it was replaced by a house. The building faced Essex Street. Mount Vernon Street is at the right in this picture. These German-made postcards often had human figures and automobiles added into the original photograph. (Photograph courtesy of the Provenzano Collection.)

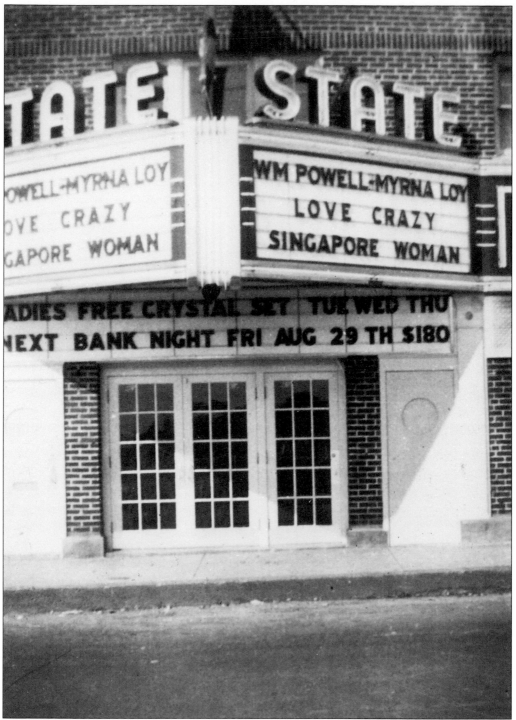

The State Theater, located at the railroad track crossing on Central Street, was Saugus' only indoor theater in the 1940s. One could see a double feature, newsreel, and cartoons for 25¢. On certain days, they even gave away free dishes. (Photograph courtesy of the Down Collection.)

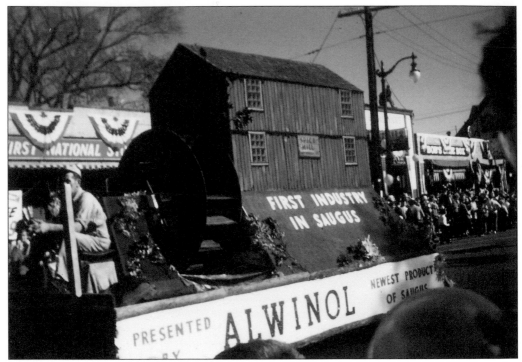

This float is part of the 325th anniversary parade in 1954. Note the First National Store in the background. It is located on Central Street in Saugus Center. (Photograph courtesy of Sylvia French, Down Collection.)

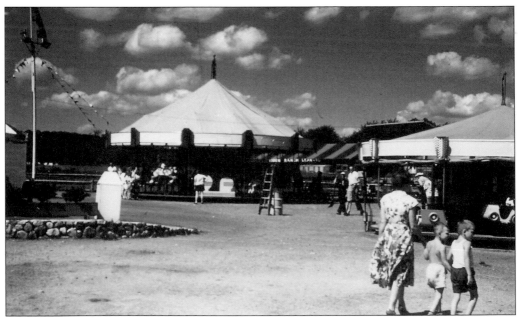

Kiddie Ranch was a small amusement park for very young children. The park was located on Route One, just south of Saugus High School. (Photograph courtesy of Paul Carlson, Carlson Collection.)

Six

Schools

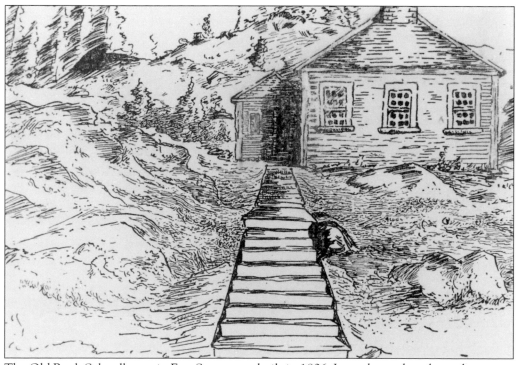

The Old Rock Schoolhouse in East Saugus was built in 1806. It was located on the rock outcrop that overlooks the junction of Chestnut Street and Lincoln Avenue. During an attempt to move it, it crashed into the street below. (Photograph courtesy of the Down Collection.)

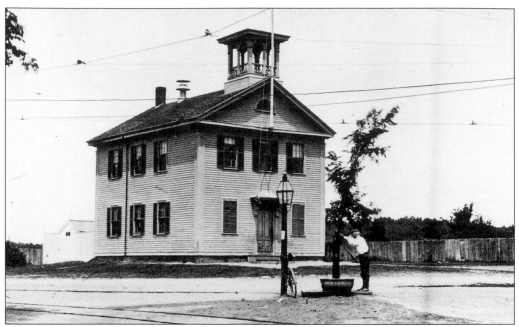

This is the North Saugus School, located at the corner of Walnut and Water Streets, *c.* 1900. Note the streetcar tracks leading to Wakefield to the left. The bicyclist is getting a drink of water from a pump; the trough was for horses. This building was later enlarged and was turned 90 degrees. It is occupied today by offices. (Photograph courtesy of the Carlson Collection.)

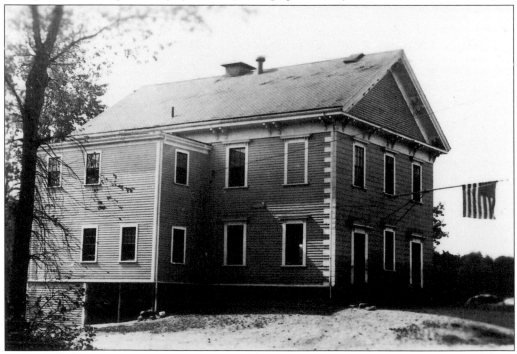

This is the original Oaklandvale School, built in the late 1800s. As a result of the development of housing tracts in the 1950s, the present Oaklandvale School was built behind this one, and this structure was torn down. (Photograph courtesy of the Carlson Collection.)

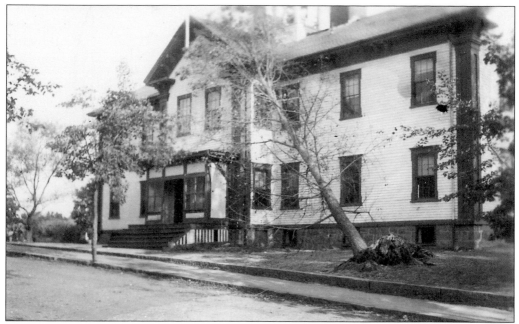

The Mansfield School was named in honor of Eliza A. Mansfield, who taught in Saugus for over fifty years. The school was located on the corner of Chestnut and Wendell Streets. This view was taken in 1938. (Photograph courtesy of Paul Carlson, Carlson Collection.)

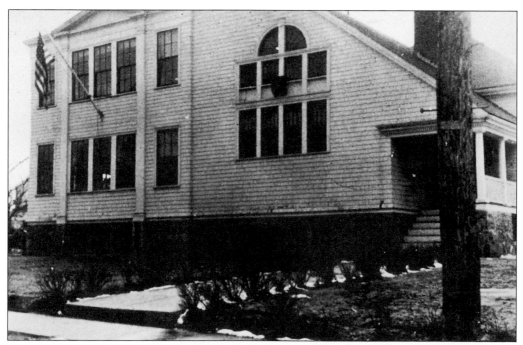

The original Lynnhurst School was located about one quarter of a mile from the present school. This view shows an addition that was built onto the left end of the original building. This building was replaced in the same program that replaced the Oaklandvale School. (Photograph courtesy of the Down Collection.)

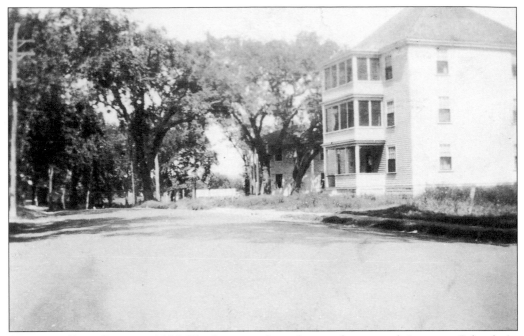

We are on Essex Street in 1925. The house at the right was the original Armitage School. As a school, it was a two-story building that stood on the west side of Essex Street. When the brick school, now Armitage Apartments, was built, this structure was moved to the other side of the street, a third floor was added, and it became a house. (Photograph courtesy of Anna Peterson, Down Collection.)

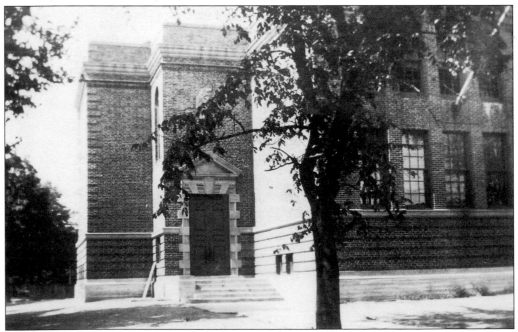

This is the brick Armitage School in 1925. It and several other elementary schools were closed in the early 1980s as a result of the passage of Proposition 2 1/2. This is now an apartment building. (Photograph courtesy of Anna Peterson, Down Collection.)

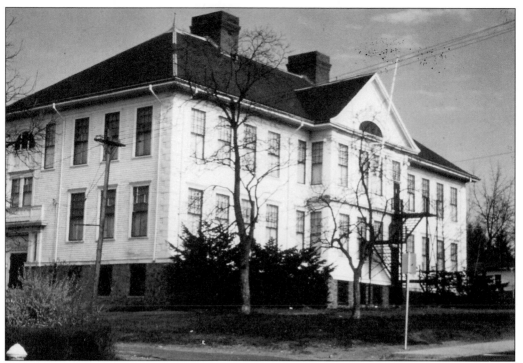

The Felton School, named for Cornelius Conway Felton, stood on Central Street opposite the end of School Street. It was torn down in 1982, when a main support beam was found to be a quarter of an inch from slipping out of position. This site is now being developed for a new Senior Center. (Photograph courtesy of Norman Down.)

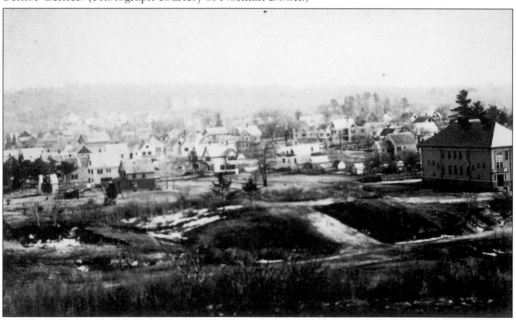

This overview of Hurd Avenue (in the foreground) shows the rear of the Felton School at the right. The excavated area along Hurd Avenue was a clay pit until the Veterans' Memorial School was built on the site in the early 1950s. (Photograph courtesy of the Down Collection.)

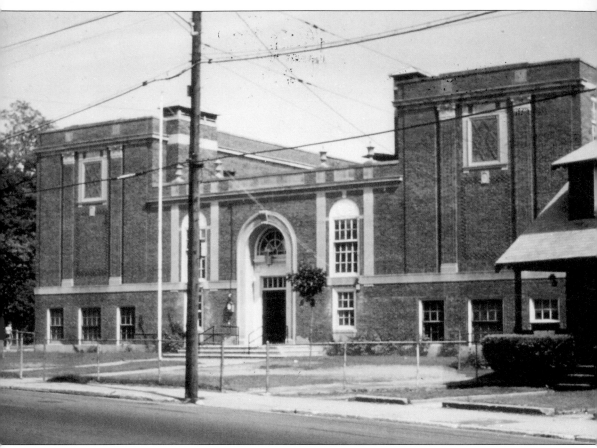

The Sweetser School was located on Lincoln Avenue at the corner of Baker Street. Earlier, this location had been the site of the wooden Lincoln School. Closed following the passage of Proposition 2 1/2, this building was torn down to make way for the Sweetser's Corner Senior Housing. (Photograph courtesy of Norman Down.)

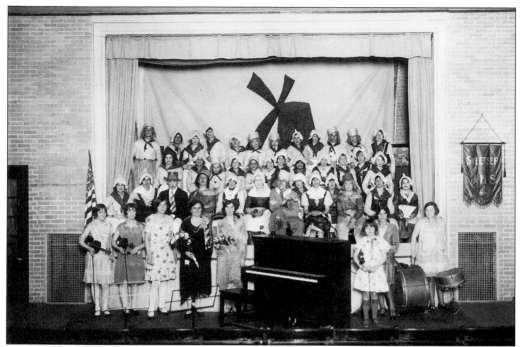

The children of the Sweetser Junior High School (grades 7 and 8) pose on the stage in the auditorium (year and event are unknown). (Photograph courtesy of Leon C. Young, Down Collection.)

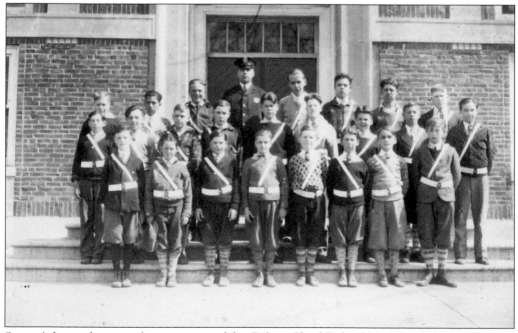

Saugus' first safety patrol was organized by Police Chief Roland A. Mansfield Jr. in 1929. Essentially, they were crossing guards in an era when automobile traffic was not as dangerous as it is now. They are posing in front of the Sweetser School. (Photograph courtesy of the Down Collection.)

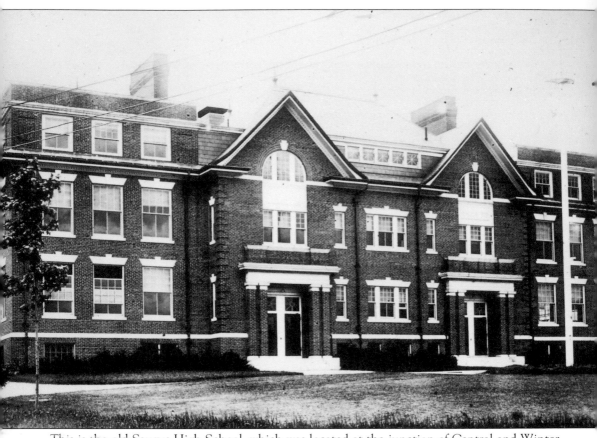

This is the old Saugus High School, which was located at the junction of Central and Winter Streets in Saugus Center. Built in 1906, it was later used as a junior high school. (Photograph courtesy of the Down Collection.)

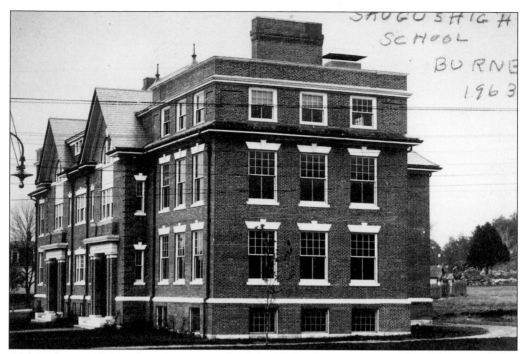

Although an addition, later known as the Evans School, was constructed on the rear of this building, the Saugus High School is shown here before any additions were built. (Photograph courtesy of the Down Collection.)

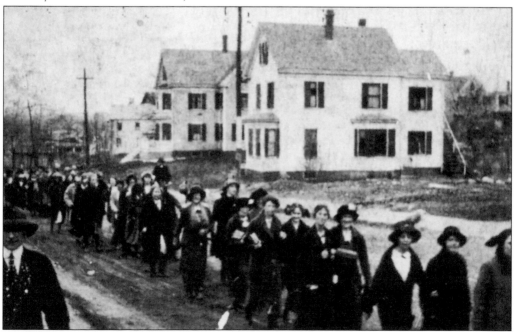

These students are marching to protest the firing of their high school principal, Mr. James A. Butterworth. Supposedly, he was too lenient with the pupils. When Police Chief Roland Mansfield found out his daughter was in the demonstration, it is said that he angrily sent her home. This activity took place around 1915. (Photograph courtesy of the Down Collection.)

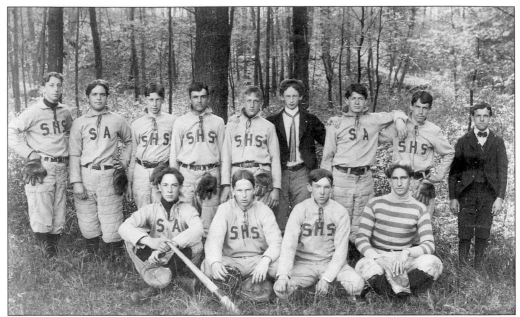

Here is a Saugus High baseball team, c. 1905. The team is listed by last name as follows: McKenzie (captain and shortstop), Hitchings (second base), Cann (first base), Dodge (third base), Edwards (left field), Strout (substitute), Morris (substitute), Coombs (substitute), Libby (right field), Upham (pitcher), Fiske (catcher), McCullough (center field), Chadwick (manager), and Morse (scorer). (Photograph courtesy of Phyllis E. Spidell, Down Collection.)

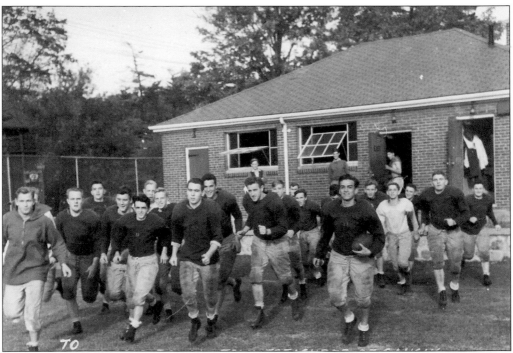

Here, one of Saugus' powerhouse football teams of the 1940s leaves the locker room at Stackpole Field. (Photograph courtesy of Phyllis Spidell, Down Collection.)

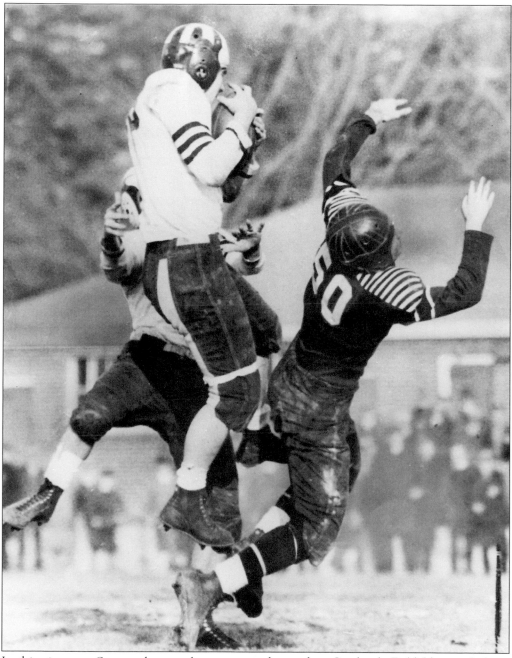

In this picture, a Saugus player makes a spectacular catch at Stackpole Field (date and player unknown). (Photograph courtesy of Phyllis Spidell, Down Collection.)

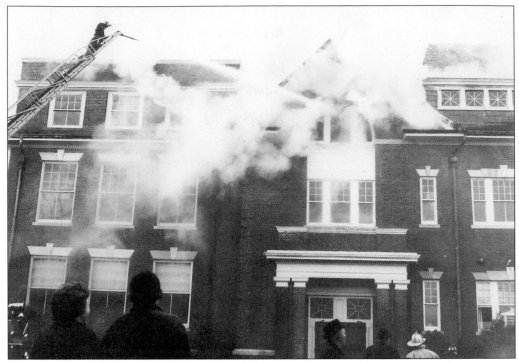

The old Saugus High School was destroyed by arson in 1963. The fire was set by a disturbed student who subsequently damaged two more schools. (Photograph courtesy of Edward Caffarella, Middle School Collection.)

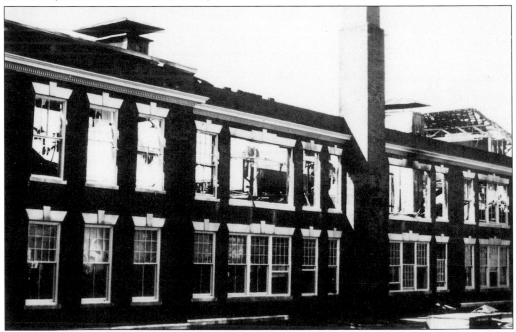

This is the aftermath of the junior high (the old high school) fire in October 1963. As a result of this destruction, the Belmonte Middle School was built on Dow Street. (Photograph courtesy of the Down Collection.)

Seven

The Rustic Life

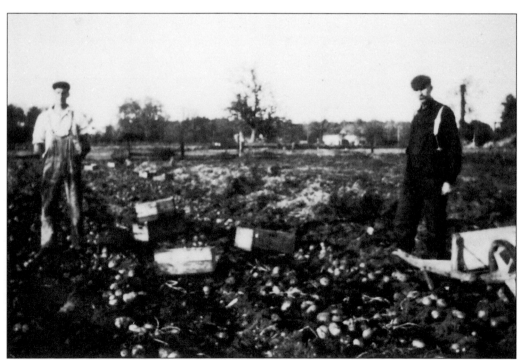

For most of its history, Saugus was primarily farmland. From 1900 on, it became increasingly a residential suburb of Boston. (Photograph courtesy of the Down Collection.)

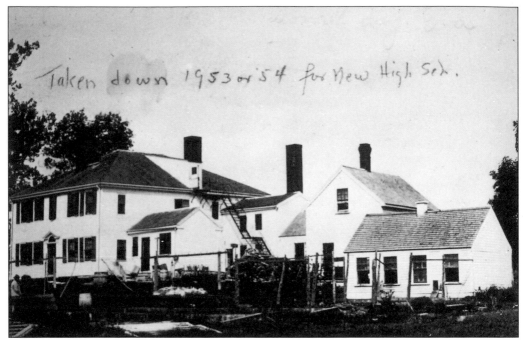

Taken down 1953 or '54 for New High Sch.

The Town Poor Farm (formerly the William Tudor summer estate) was located on Route One at the intersection with Main Street. It was taken down in the early 1950s when the present Saugus High School was built. (Photograph courtesy of the Down Collection.)

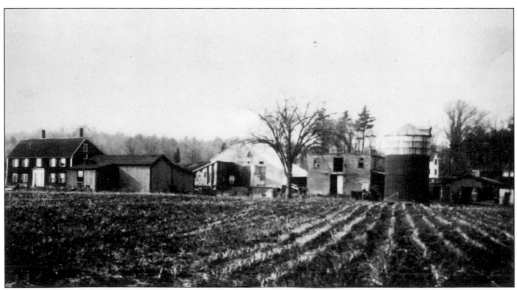

The Howlett Farm in North Saugus is shown here in the late 1800s. Saugus had small produce and dairy farms until the 1950s. (Photograph courtesy of the Down Collection.)

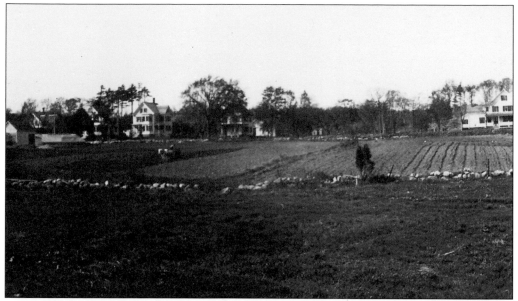

This was the Holmes Farm, located between Highland Avenue and Main Street and near Route One. (Photograph courtesy of the Down Collection.)

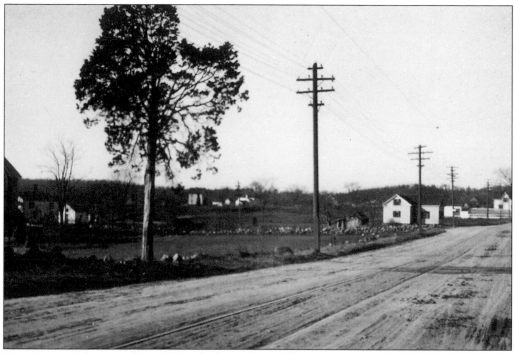

The photographer is on Main Street looking toward Highland Avenue. The nearest house is on the corner of Vine and Main Streets. (Photograph courtesy of the Down Collection.)

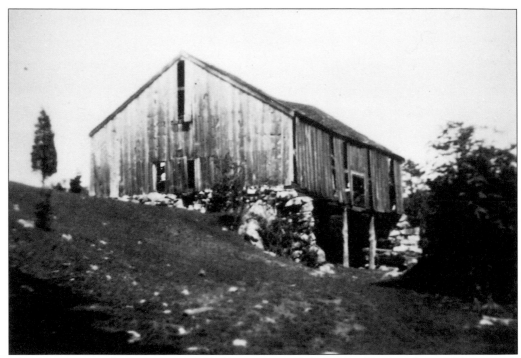

This barn in North Saugus was probably on one of the many Hawkes farms. (Photograph courtesy of the Down Collection.)

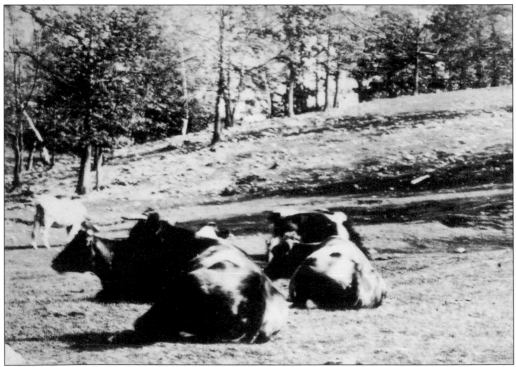

Frank Fiske's dairy herd is shown here, lounging in the field along School Street. The farmland was sold for housing in the 1950s. (Photograph courtesy of the Down Collection.)

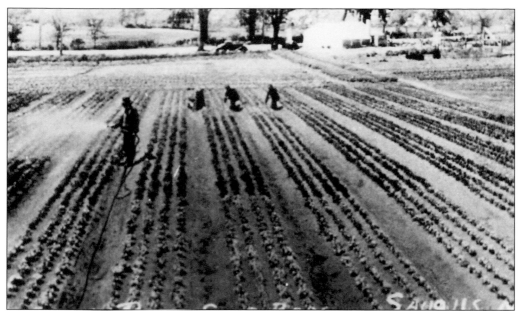

Gordon's pansy farm was located between Vine Street and Route One. The highway runs across the far background of the picture. (Photograph courtesy of the Down Collection.)

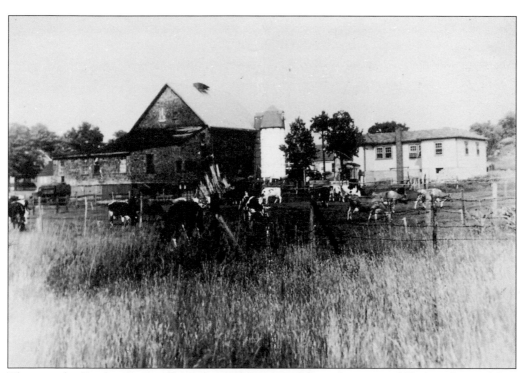

This was the Stocker-Rutten Farm, located between Adams Avenue and Denver Street. Most of the pasture land is now property owned by the Middle School. (Photograph courtesy of the Down Collection.)

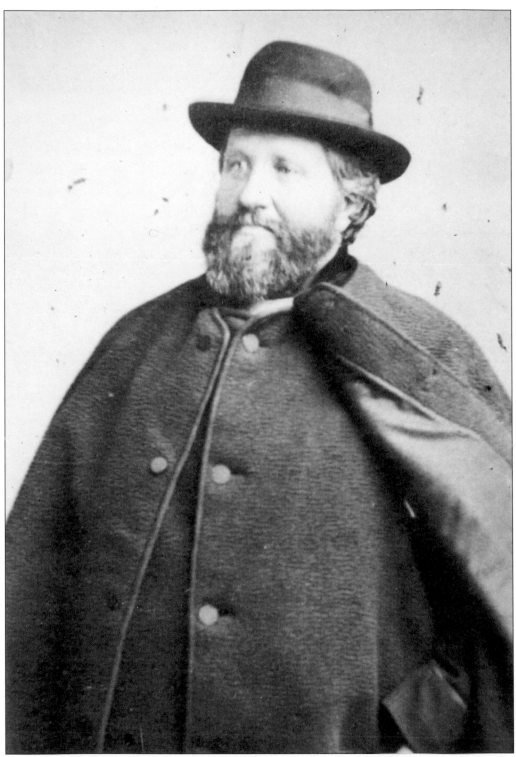

Dr. William Sawyer, a dentist, owned an ice house on Pranker's Pond. It was located at the corner of Appleton and Summer Streets. (Photograph courtesy of the Down Collection.)

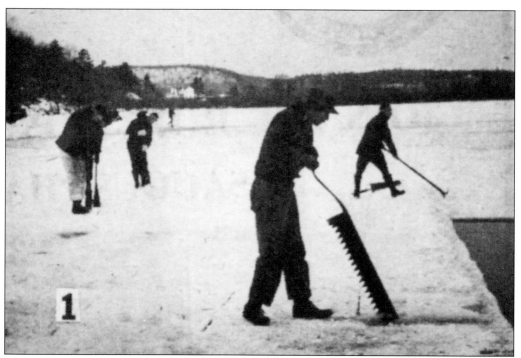

These men are cutting ice with handsaws on Pranker's Pond. As the pond became silted up and choked with pond lilies, it came to gradually be referred to as Lily Pond. The original pond disappeared when the dam was dynamited in the 1950s. (Photograph courtesy of the Down Collection.)

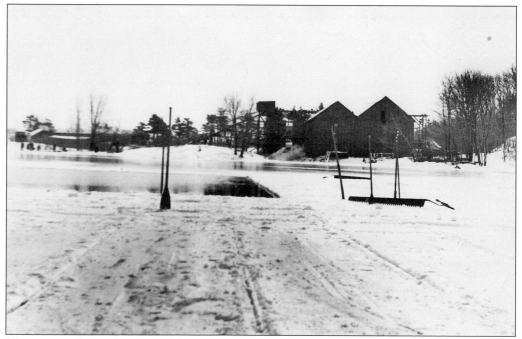

Here we see the implements of the ice cutters. One of the many ice houses and its ramp can be seen in the background. (Photograph courtesy of the Carlson Collection.)

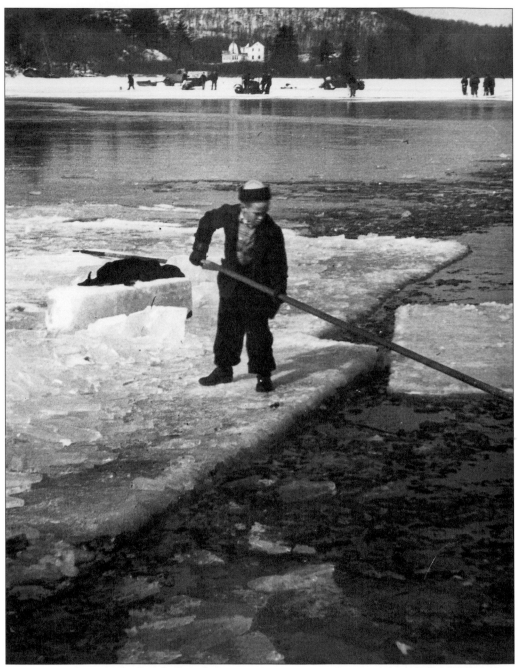

Many young boys worked with their fathers in the ice cutting business. This lad is poling an ice block through a channel cut in the ice toward the ice house ramp. (Photograph courtesy of the Carlson Collection.)

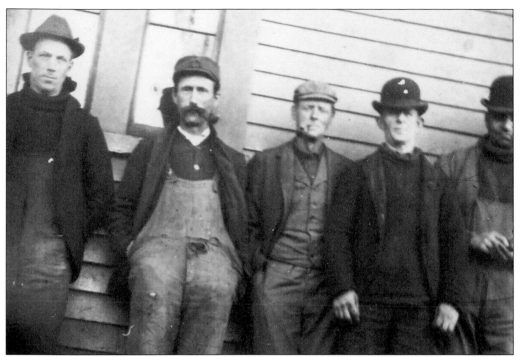

Here is an ice cutting crew, c. 1900. One of the men is identified as Joseph MacGilvery. (Photograph courtesy of the Down Collection.)

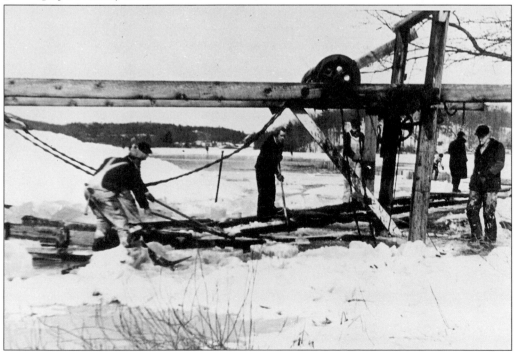

Here we see ice blocks being set into place for the trip up the ramp. The ramp led to a scaffold on the side of the building from which the ice slides down a chute into the ice house. (Photograph courtesy of the Down Collection.)

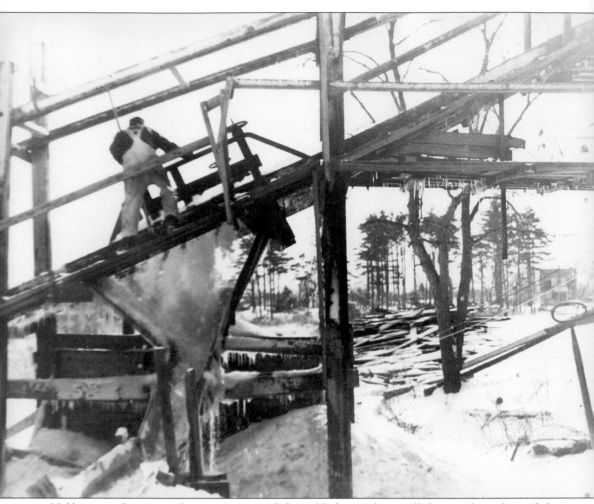

Halfway up the ramp, there was a set of sharp blades to shave off the rough surface of the ice. One workman slipped into the blades and was so severely cut that he died. (Photograph courtesy of the Down Collection.)

The ice block is poled into position for its trip up the ramp. (Photograph courtesy of the Down Collection.)

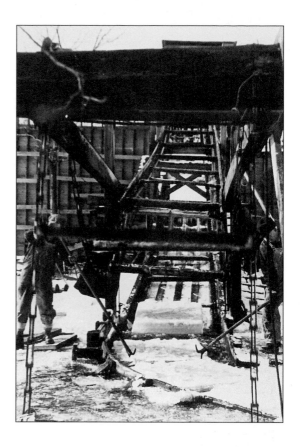

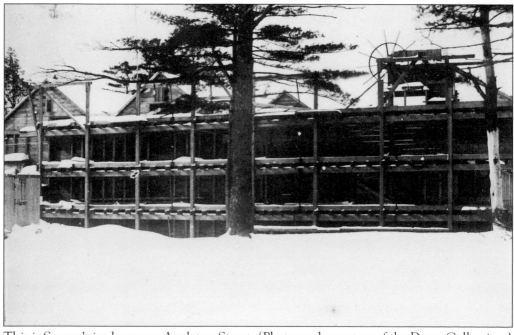

This is Sawyer's ice house on Appleton Street. (Photograph courtesy of the Down Collection.)

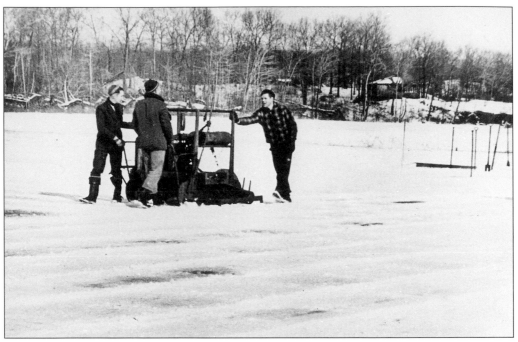

Ice cutting was made easier with the invention of the gasoline-powered saw. This photo was taken around 1930. (Photograph courtesy of Richard Provenzano.)

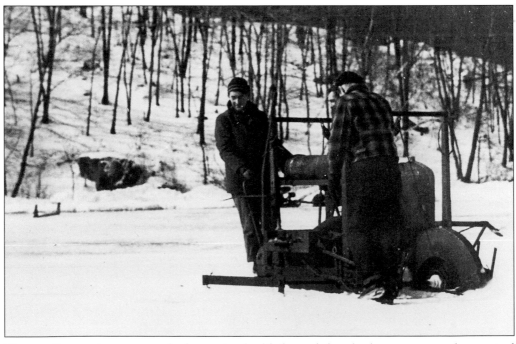

The gasoline engine was attached to a circular blade, and then both were mounted on a steel frame which could then slide across the ice. (Photograph courtesy of the Down Collection.)

Eight

Transportation: Way to Go

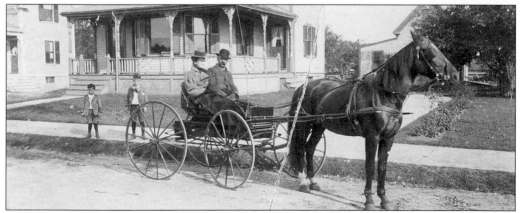

The Dodge family is seen here posed in front of their house at 26 Summer Street in the late 1890s. From left to right are: Arthur, Harold, Harriet, and Herbert. Harold later served Saugus as town accountant, school committee member, and selectman. He also served as town treasurer for 27 years until his retirement in 1954. (Photograph courtesy of Phyllis Spidell, Down Collection.)

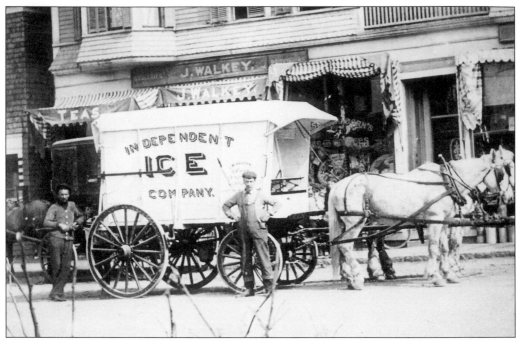

At the turn of the century, most products were delivered directly to the home, using horse-drawn wagons. (Photograph courtesy of the Down Collection.)

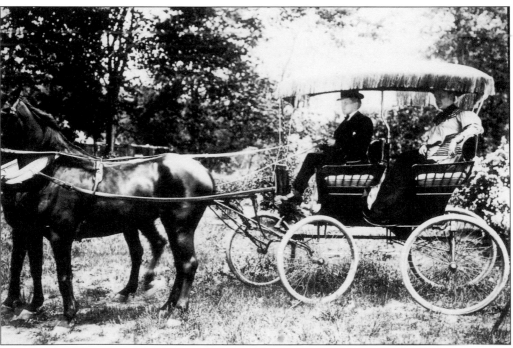

The wealthy folks often rode about in carriages like this one. It is a surrey. The design originated in Surrey, England.

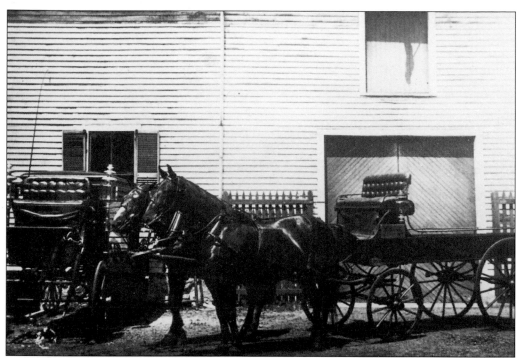

Here are a wagon and a horse-drawn hearse, owned by the Bisbee Funeral Home at 549 Lincoln Avenue. (Photograph courtesy of the Provenzano Collection.)

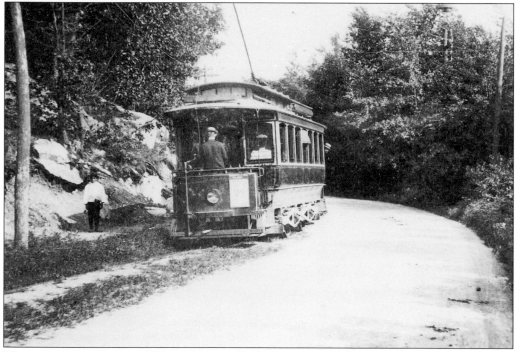

This streetcar is shown on Water Street, which connects North Saugus with Wakefield. The streetcar used to stop and pick up milk near the O'Brien home on Walnut Street. (Photograph courtesy of the Carlson Collection.)

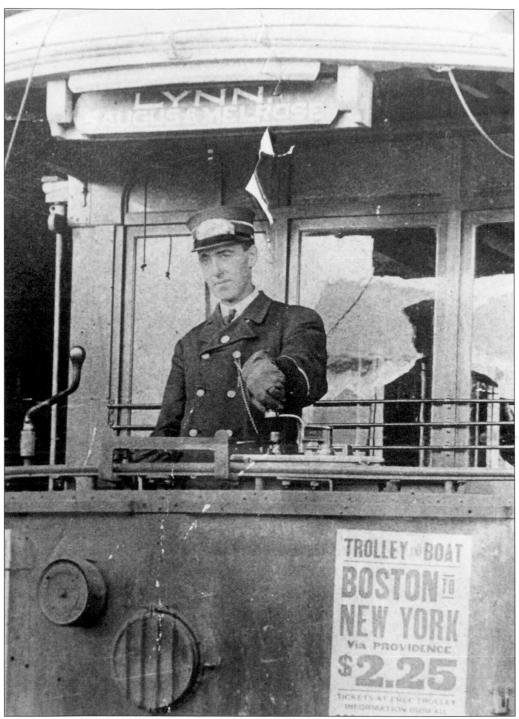

Here is a proud motorman at the controls of car 1217. This exposed position could be brutal in winter weather. Eventually, Massachusetts passed a law requiring that the motorman's platform be enclosed. This became known as the "Boston front." The car is a 1910 product of the Stephenson Car Company. (Photograph courtesy of the Down Collection.)

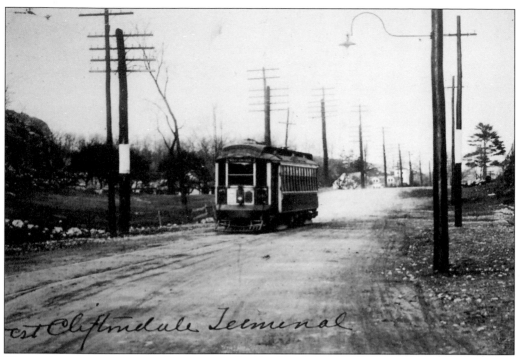

This early streetcar is waiting for a train at the Franklin Park terminal on Lincoln Avenue, near the Revere line. (Photograph courtesy of the Down Collection.)

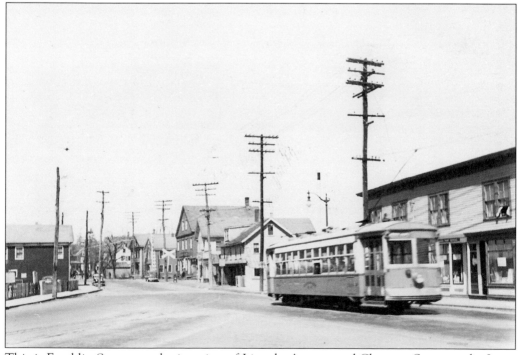

This is Franklin Square, at the junction of Lincoln Avenue and Chestnut Street at the Lynn line. The streetcar is about to cross the bridge across the Saugus River into Lynn. (Photograph courtesy of Charles A. Duncan, Carlson Collection.)

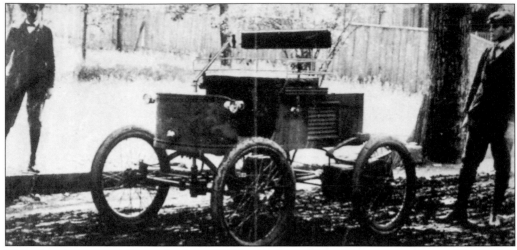

This electric automobile was built in 1897 by Professor Elihu Thompson, of Lynn. To the left is W.G. Fisher, who later went on to design automobile bodies. To the right is H.O. Westendorf. Both men worked for the General Electric Company. (Photograph courtesy of the Down Collection.)

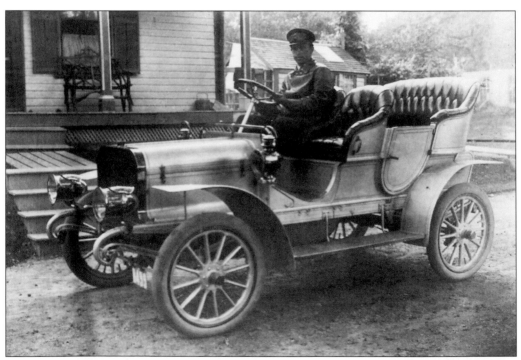

This is Frank Bosworth in an early automobile, in front of 119 Main Street, c. 1910. He was so enamored with automobiles that he later built one. (Photograph courtesy of Helen Bosworth, Down Collection.)

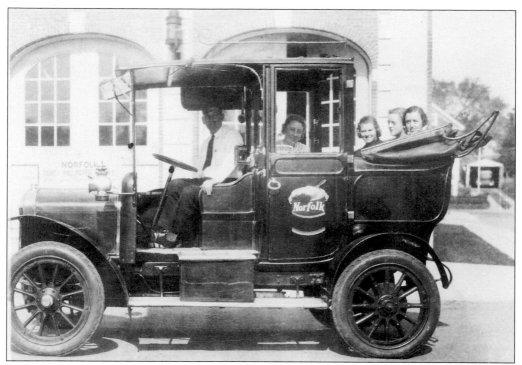

Joy-riding was a popular pastime. This photo shows Phillis Dodge (far right), Margaret Blair (second from right), and friends. The truck is labeled Norfolk Paint and Wallpaper. (Photograph courtesy of Phyllis Spidell, Down Collection.)

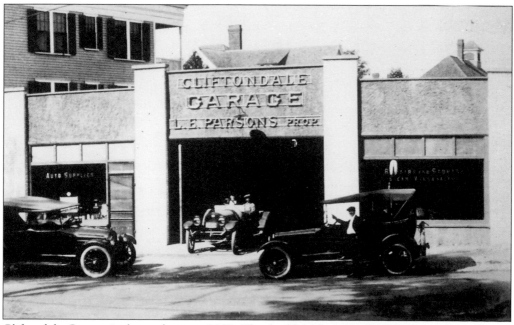

Cliftondale Garage is shown here, c. 1930. This building later became Hanson Chevrolet. A Mobil station now occupies the site. (Photograph courtesy of the Down Collection.)

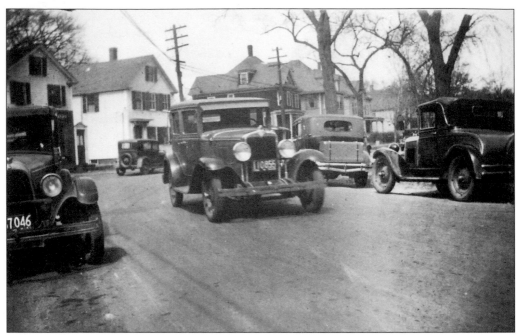

Here is Jackson Street, Cliftondale, taken sometime around 1940 from a spot near the corner of Jackson and Essex Streets. (Photograph courtesy of the Down Collection.)

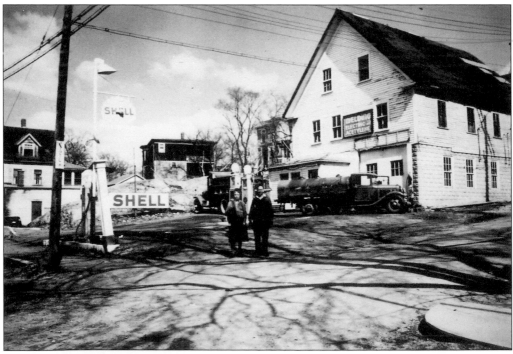

This building, at the corner of Lincoln and Fairview Avenues, has been dedicated to serving personal transportation for many years. It has been a blacksmith shop, a carriage-maker's shop, and an auto repair shop. (Photograph courtesy of the Down Collection.)

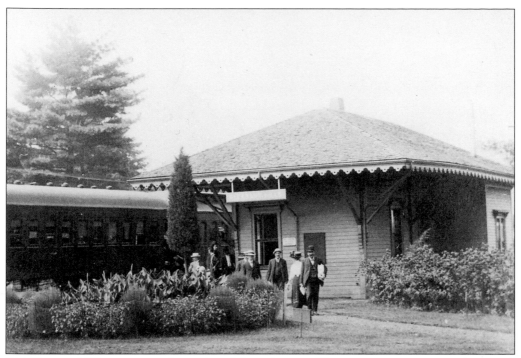

The Pleasant Hills station was located on Adams Avenue. Thirteen passenger trains once served daily the Saugus Branch. Contests were held among the B & M stationmasters to produce the most beautiful garden. The Pleasant Hills stationmaster usually won. (Photograph courtesy of the Carlson Collection.)

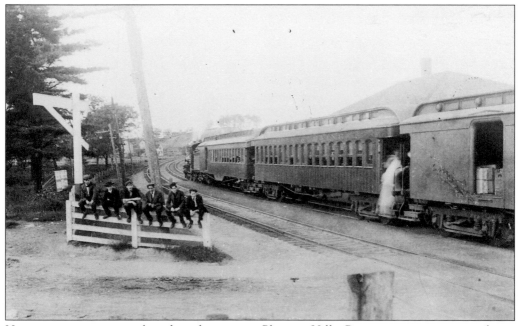

Here we see a passenger boarding the train at Pleasant Hills. Passenger service trains, always with steam engines, continued in Saugus until the mid-1950s. (Photograph courtesy of the Carlson Collection.)

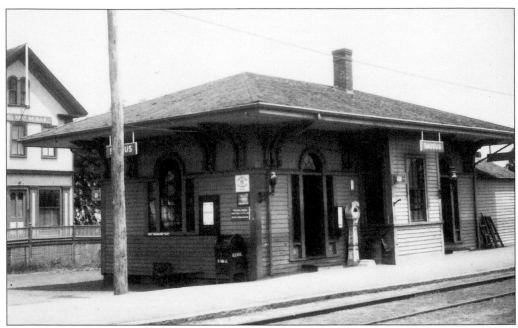

The Saugus Center railroad station was a busy place at the turn of the century. The building at the left was originally the GAR veterans' hall. It later became a hay and feed store. (Photograph courtesy of the Down Collection.)

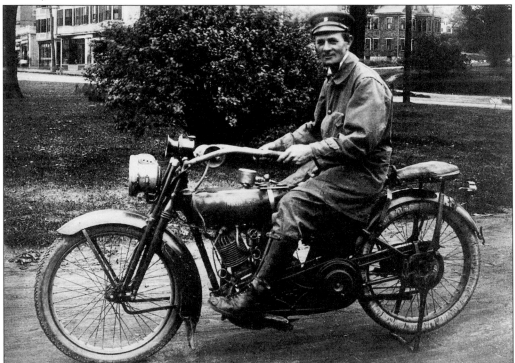

Motorcycle cops are nothing new. Patrolman James Sullivan is at the Cliftondale rotary sometime in the early 1920s. Lincoln Avenue and Smith Road can be seen in the background. (Photograph courtesy of the Carlson Collection.)

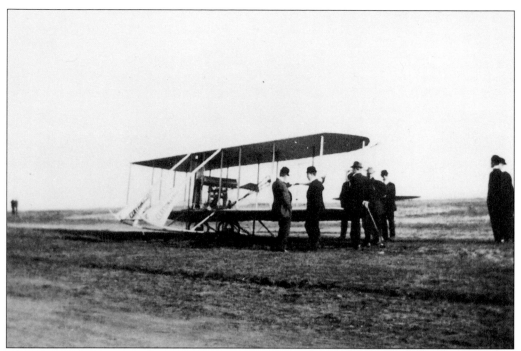

There once was a race track on the salt marsh behind Baker Hill. In the early 1900s, the track became a field used for flying. This shot was taken around 1912. (Photograph courtesy of the Carlson Collection.)

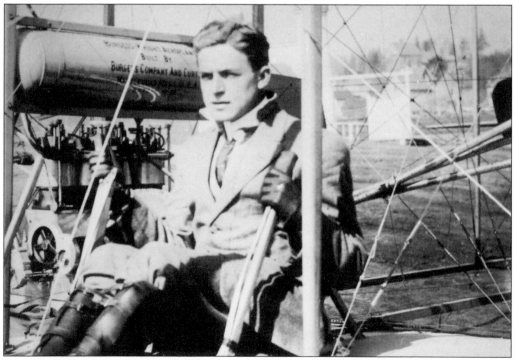

Harry A. Atwood was one the earliest aviators. He flew the first air mail from Saugus to Lynn in 1912. (Photograph courtesy of the Down Collection.)

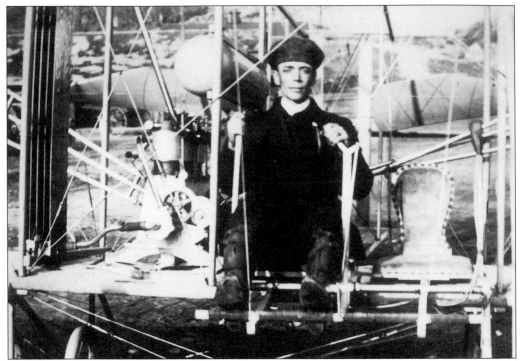

Lincoln Beachey was Atwood's partner at the time. A daredevil, he later flew a balloon over the White House. He was killed while stunt-flying in California. (Photograph courtesy of the Down Collection.)

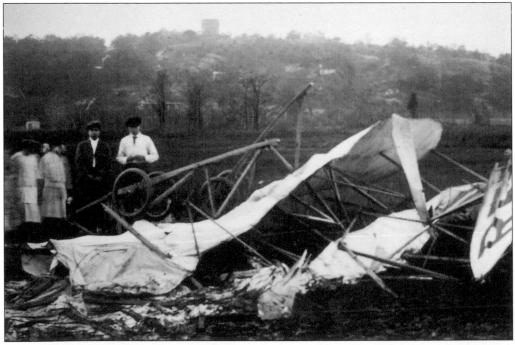

This fatal crash took place at Atwood Park on the salt marsh. Baker Hill is in the background. (Photograph courtesy of the Down Collection.)

Nine

People

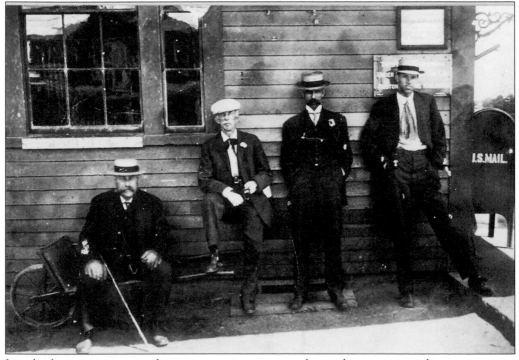

In suburban communities, the train station was as much a gathering spot as the country store was in more rural areas. This group is at the Saugus Center station. (Photograph courtesy of the Down Collection.)

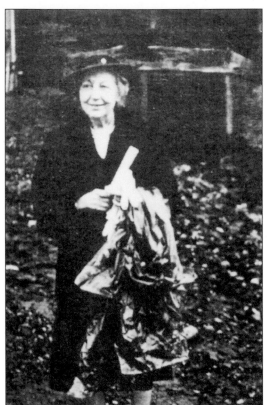

Miss Louise M. Hawkes, a descendent of one of Saugus' earliest settlers, was largely responsible for saving the Ironmaster's House. Henry Ford wanted to purchase it and move it to his Dearborn Village museum in Michigan. Miss Hawkes led the fight to keep it in Saugus. (Photograph courtesy of the Down Collection.)

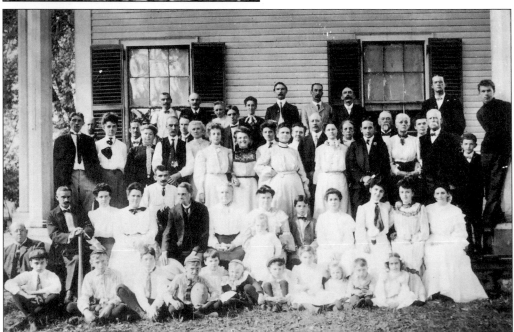

This is the Penney/Oliver/Cutter family reunion at the old Cheever House on Essex Street, c. 1903. The Penney family owned the house at the time. (Photograph courtesy of the Down Collection.)

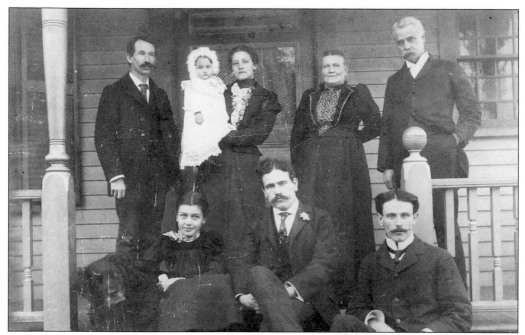

These folks are the Kennedy family, who lived on the corner of Tuttle and Essex Streets. From left to right are: (front row) Agnes, William, and Frank Kennedy; (back row) Joseph F. Neale, Doris Neale, Bess (Kennedy) Neale, Margaret Kennedy, and James Kennedy. (Photograph courtesy of Phyllis E. Spidell, Down Collection.)

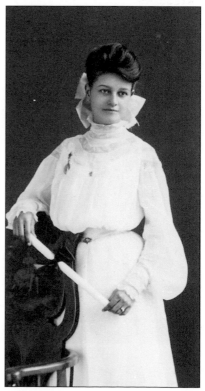

Agnes B. Kennedy graduated from Saugus High in 1904. She later married Harold Dodge and had three children. She died in 1959. (Photograph courtesy of Phyllis E. Spidell, Down Collection.)

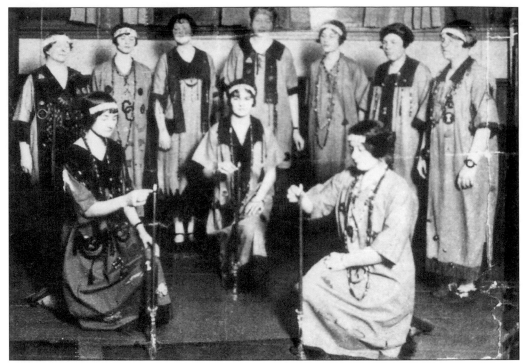

Many early clubs and youth groups focused on "Indian" themes. This is a group of Campfire Girls. Former Saugus teacher Gwendoline Walters is shown at the left. (Photograph courtesy of the Down Collection.)

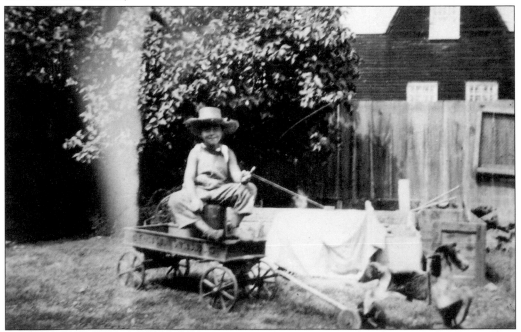

This is Amos Cutter playing in the backyard of the Mansfield House on Central Street, c. 1910. Note the Ironmaster's House in the background. (Photograph courtesy of the Cutter Family, Down Collection.)

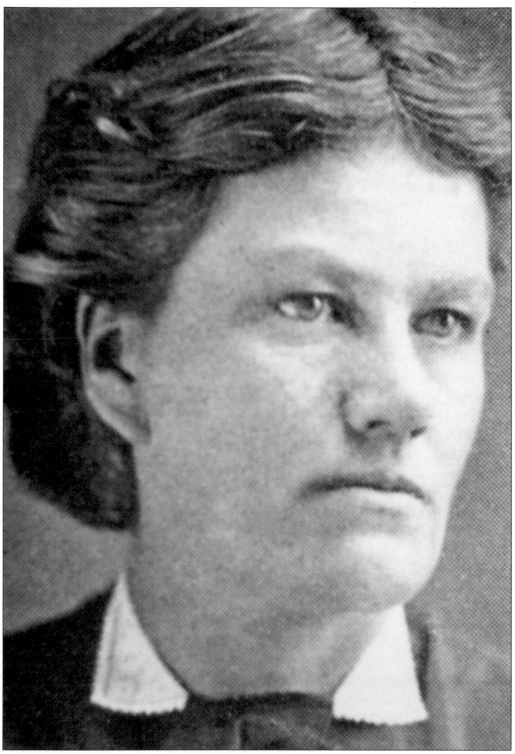

Miss Mary Newhall was the first Sunday school teacher at the Cliftondale Methodist Church. (Photograph courtesy of the Down Collection.)

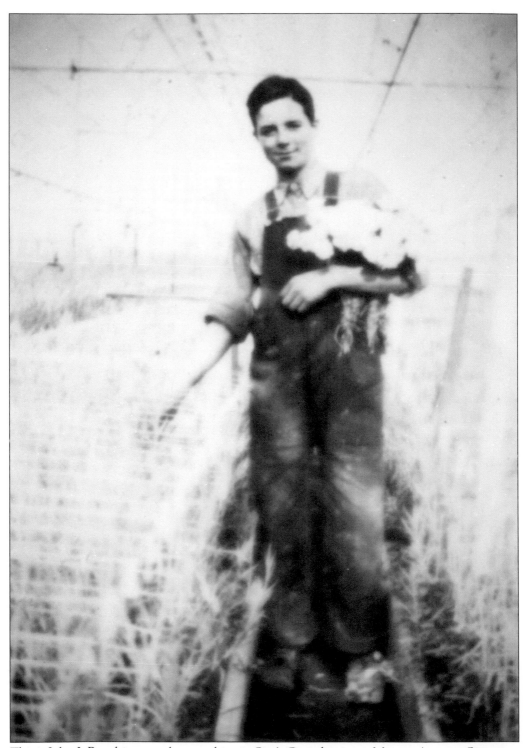

This is John J. Bucchiere as a boy, working in Sim's Greenhouse on Morton Avenue. Sim was a major producer of carnations. Mr. Bucchiere later became a selectman in Saugus. (Photograph courtesy of the Down Collection.)

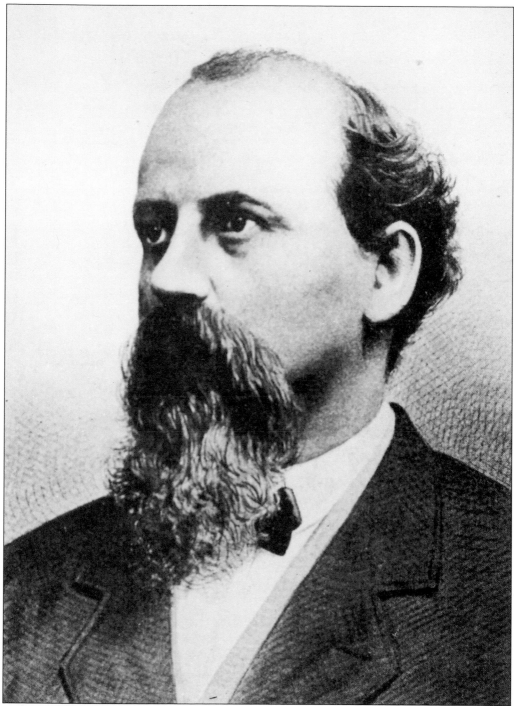

Saugus native Gustavus Vasa Fox (1821–1883) was undersecretary of the Navy, under Presidents Lincoln and Johnson. As such, he helped to develop the Civil War ironclad ships known as monitors. He saw to it that one of them was named the USS *Saugus*. Later, as Ambassador Plenipotentiary to Russia's court of Alexander II, he negotiated the Alaska Purchase for just over $7 million in 1876. (Photograph courtesy of the Down Collection.)

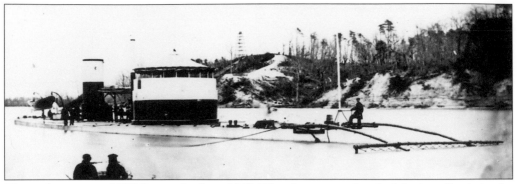

This is the monitor USS *Saugus*, built in 1862. The photo was taken by Matthew Brady in the James River, Virginia. (Photograph courtesy of the National Archives.)

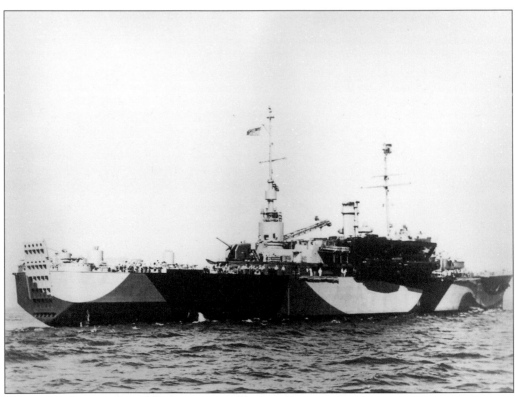

This is the troop carrier USS *Saugus*, one of many ships to carry the name. Gustavus Fox was responsible for making sure that there will always be a USS *Saugus*. (Photograph courtesy of the Down Collection.)

Ten

The Newburyport Turnpike: Route One

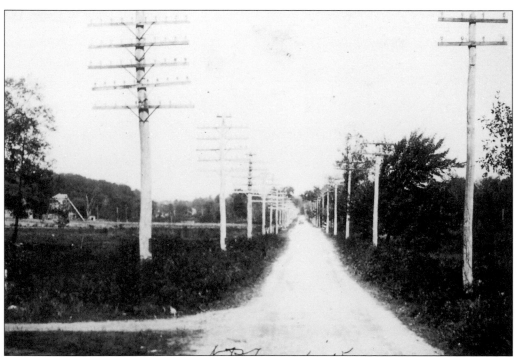

Here is the Newburyport Turnpike (Route One) in Saugus, at the turn of the century. The road was finished around 1805. In 1915, historian Horace Atherton questioned the wisdom of building it by saying, "it certainly has never benefited Saugus much and has always been of endless expense." Today, the businesses along Route One generate millions of dollars in taxes for Saugus. (Photograph courtesy of the Down Collection.)

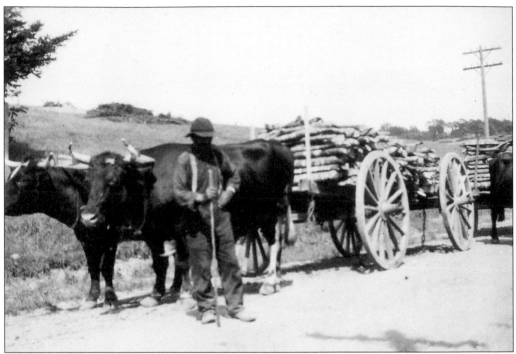

The Newburyport Turnpike was built in as nearly a straight line as possible, to connect Newburyport with Boston. This ox-cart load of wood is typical of the early traffic. (Photograph courtesy of the Down Collection.)

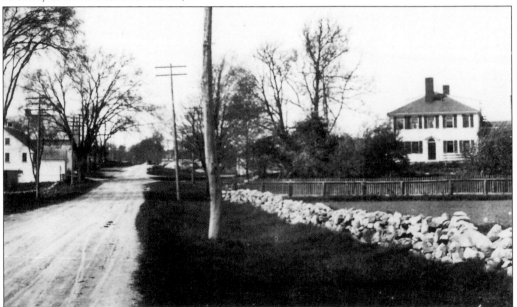

William Tudor, a Boston lawyer, built a summer estate on the turnpike at the junction of Main Street. He named it "Rockwood." The property later became the Town Poor Farm. The house was located on the site of the present football practice field at Saugus High. Tudor's son Frederick became so wealthy selling ice that he became known as "The Ice King." (Photograph courtesy of the Down Collection.)

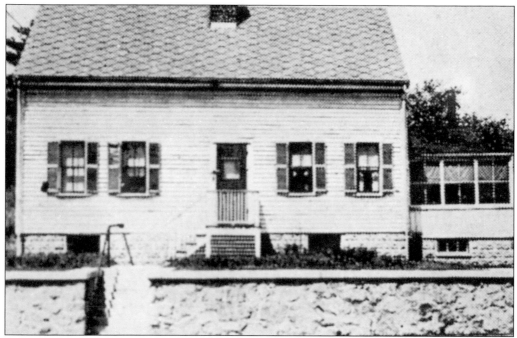

This was a toll house on the turnpike, located at what is now the junction of Routes 1 and 99. It was tended by the Felton family. A son, Cornelius, later became a Greek scholar and a president of Harvard University. (Photograph courtesy of the Down Collection.)

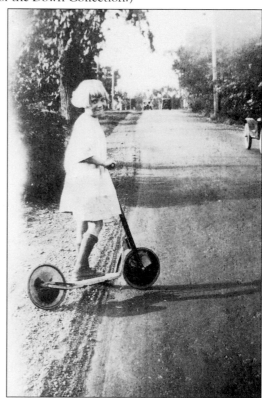

Try crossing Route One on a scooter today! Ina Eckstrom did it on August 24, 1925. (Photograph courtesy of Anna Peterson, Down Collection.)

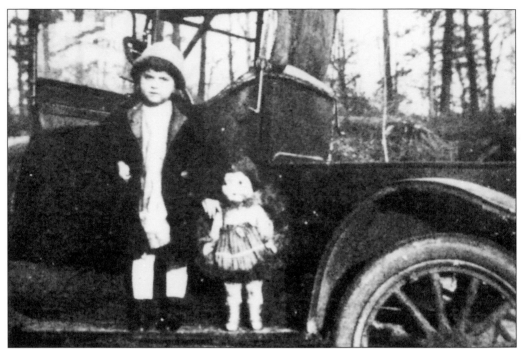

The development of the "horseless carriage" brought new life to the Newburyport Turnpike. (Photograph courtesy of the Down Collection.)

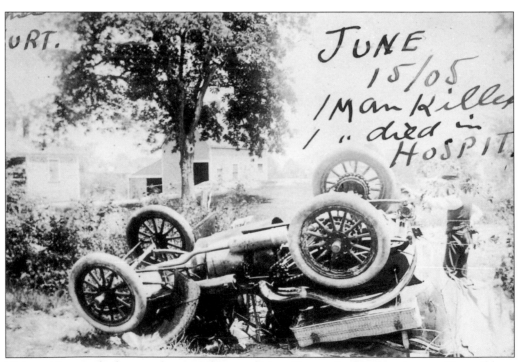

This accident took place on the turnpike, near Felton Street. At this time, it was still possible to enter the highway from Felton Street. (Photograph courtesy of the Down Collection.)

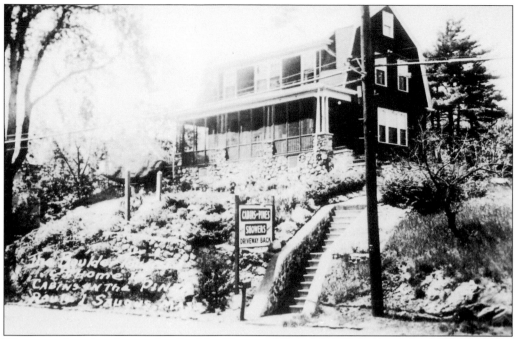

The sign identifies this as the Boulder Tourists Home, Cabins in the Pines, Route One. It was located on the northbound side between Main and Walnut Streets (date unknown). (Photograph courtesy of the Provenzano Collection.)

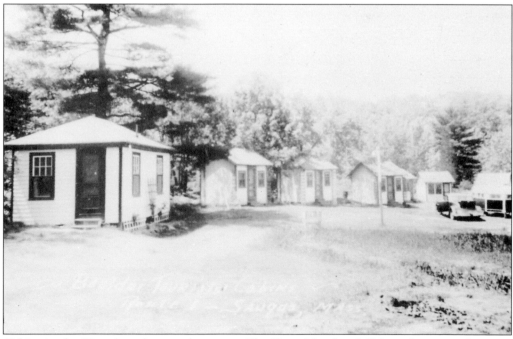

Cabins in the Pines later became known as The Pines Motel and Cabins. It acquired quite a seedy reputation. (Photograph courtesy of the Provenzano Collection.)

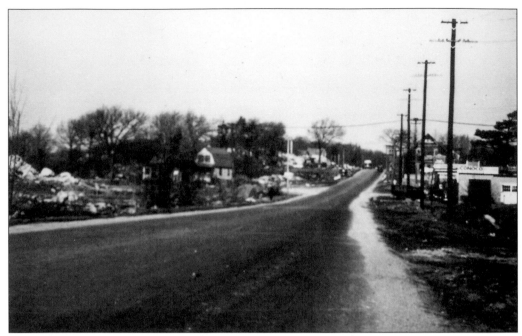

Here we are looking north, toward the Main Street intersection. Note that there is no overpass. Also note the amount of traffic! (Photograph courtesy of the Down Collection.)

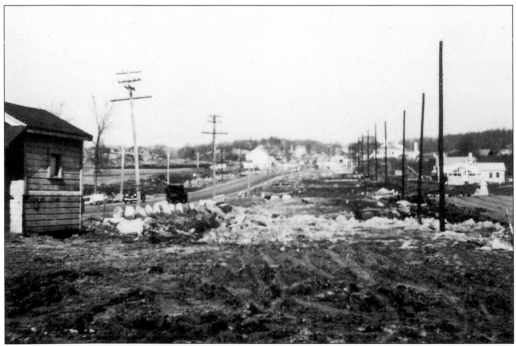

The state is widening Route One in 1933. We are looking north, from Essex Street toward Main Street. The Town Farm can be seen at the right in the distance. The overpasses were built at this time. (Photograph courtesy of the Down Collection.)

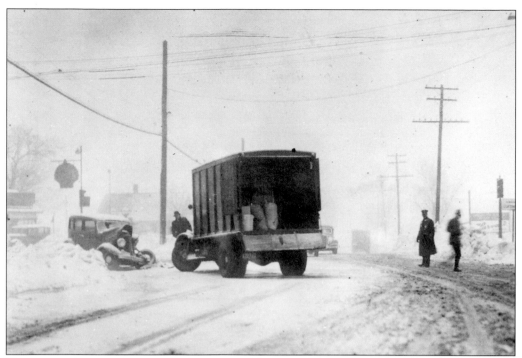

Here is another accident scene, this time at Essex Street in the early 1930s. Note the traffic light on the right. (Photograph courtesy of the Down Collection.)

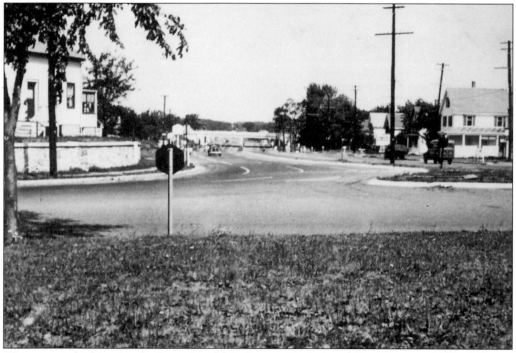

This view is looking north, from the old DeFranzo Circle (now the junction of Routes 1 and 99). The Felton Toll House is on the left, and the Essex Street overpass is in the distance. (Photograph courtesy of the Down Collection.)

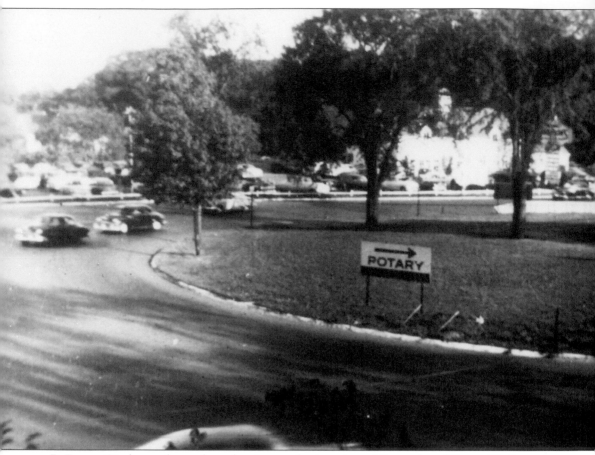

DeFranzo Circle was located at what is now the junction of Route 1 and Route 99. For years, it was the scene of many spectacular crashes. The circle was eliminated in the 1950s and replaced by an overpass further south. The building in the background was a Howard Johnson's restaurant. (Photograph courtesy of the Down Collection.)

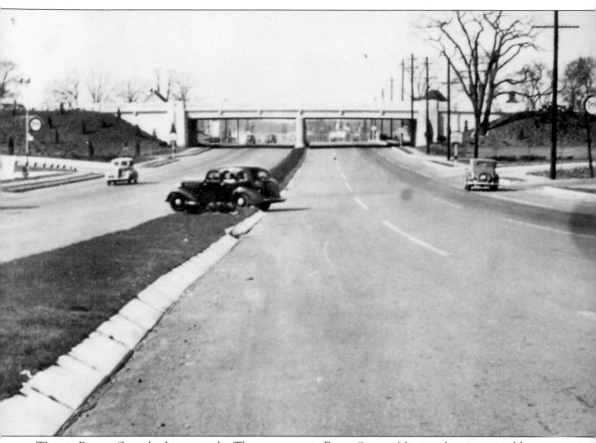

This is Route One, looking north. The overpass is Essex Street. Notice that cars could cut across the divider strip. This practice became so dangerous that the "cut-throughs" were later closed. (Photograph courtesy of the Down Collection.)

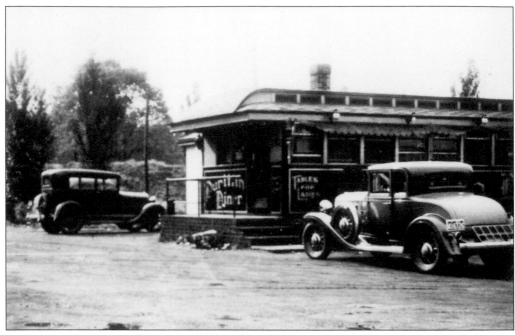

The Puritan Diner, later known as the Turnpike Diner, was located at the intersection of Route One and Walnut Street. It is believed to have been built by the Worcester Lunch Car Company of Worcester, Massachusetts. (Photograph courtesy of the Down Collection.)

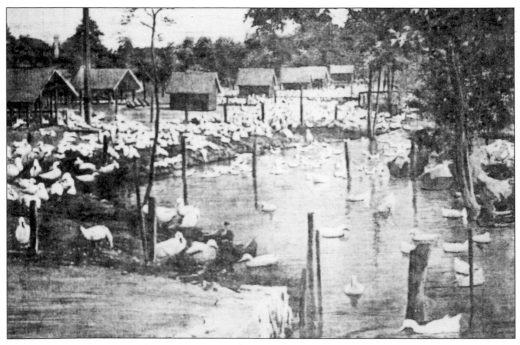

Carl's Duck Farm, owned by Carl Demauro, was on the northbound side of Route One, near the Walnut Street intersection. There was also a restaurant that served duck dinners. (Photograph courtesy of the Down Collection.)

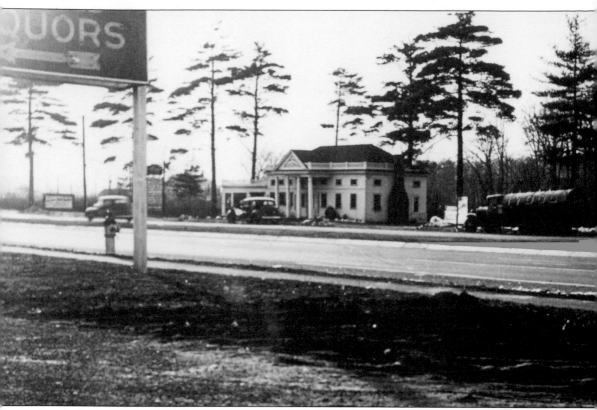

The White House restaurant stood where the Prince of Pizza is now located. (Photograph courtesy of the Down Collection.)

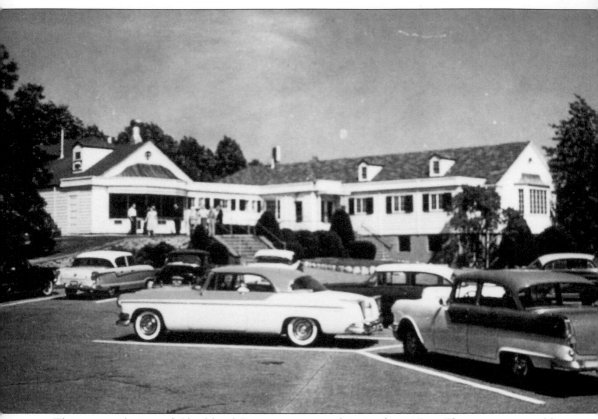

This postcard view of Chickland Restaurant was taken in the 1950s. The owners were Vic and Cliff Crawford, who also owned ViCliff's Restaurant. This Route 99 site has also been the location of Chateau de Ville, The Palace, and now, Oxygen 2. As you walked up to the front door of Chickland, you could see chickens roasting on a large set of rotisseries. (Photograph courtesy of the Provenzano Collection.)

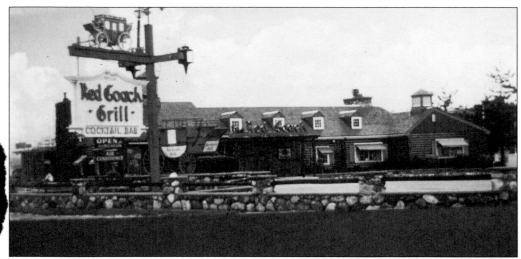

The Red Coach Grille, part of a chain of restaurants owned by the Howard Johnson Corporation, was located at the junction of Route One and the Lynn Fells Parkway. Later, it became an El Toritos restaurant. The site is now occupied by Kelly's Roast Beef. (Photograph courtesy of the Provenzano Collection.)

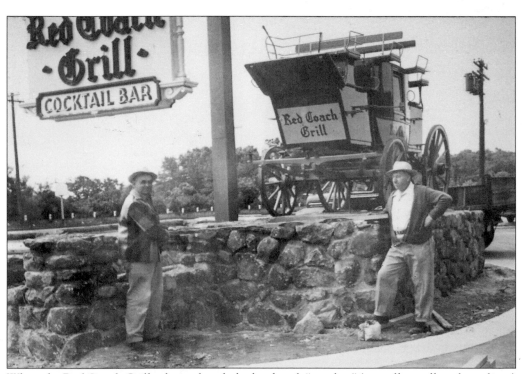

When the Red Coach Grille chain closed, the landmark "coaches" (actually small-scale replicas) were sold. (Photograph courtesy of the Down Collection.)

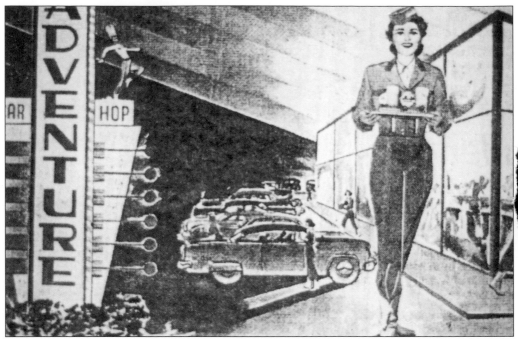

Radio personality Arnie "Woo Woo" Ginsburg advertised the Adventure Car Hop as "the place to go." It was located on the northbound side of Route One near Walnut Street. The Diplomat now occupies the site. (Photograph courtesy of the Down Collection.)

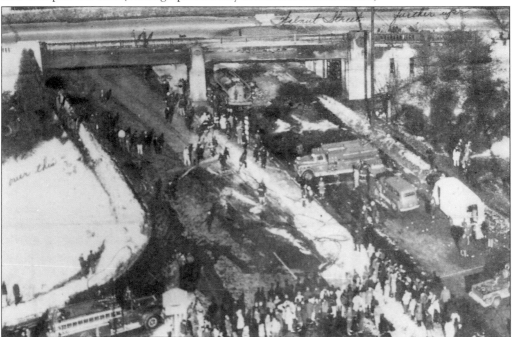

Two drivers were killed, and a bus load of Saugus High School students narrowly escaped death by incineration when a gasoline truck crashed and burned under the Walnut Street overpass in 1963. What looks like snow in this photo is actually foam. Special fire trucks were sent from Logan airport to battle this blaze. (Photograph courtesy of the Down Collection.)